THE UNITED STATES VS ALFREDO MARTINEZ

Ronald Sosinski

ARTVOICES BOOKS

INTROD

Alfredo, *the early years* by Jonathan Goldstein

Alfredo was one of my very best friends. We traveled together, plotted, planned and schemed together I was as much a part of his family and story as he was a part of my own.

One of the few things I've ever found that qualifies an artist to be an artist is that they do it as a compulsion, making art, whatever format the art might be, is not something they want to do, it us something they HAVE to do, with obsessive focus on achieving this single goal. It's as much a part of their nature as living and breathing might be.

Based upon this qualification alone Alfrerdo Martinez was the artist's artist. His obsession and focus on the things he was doing was complete and absolute. He would stay up for days at a time to finish a piece once he got started, fabricating Giant Robots from literally nothing, creating entire installation over the course of a few short days with no planning whatsoever. It was pure art what he did, it sprang from him fully formed like Athena from the mind of Zeus.

He was not receptive to many ideas about how his art should progress, even from his closest friends. I would occasionally try to steer him into what I thought might be more productive and salable paths which were, more often than not, met with willful disregard. The one small victory I might claim over Alfredo's art career was fostering an understanding that it was easier to sell flatwork rather than sculpture but honestly, he would most likely have gotten there in the end, even without my constant haranguing. He rarely ever entertained ideas about new series of works, even from me. His was a heuristically closed circuit of need, desire and achievement.

When I first met him, Alfredo was one of a group of hardcore punk kids who would hang out during the afternoons at the Aztec Lounge, in the East Village. I was working there at the time and with very little to do during these daytime shifts we somehow got talking and struck up a friendship.

What we talked about back then was overwhelmingly the things that we hoped to do. For Alfredo that was making claymation movies, an idea he was obsessed with at the time and for me it was making music.

UCTION

I thought he was a bit of a dreamer but interesting nonetheless, smart, funny, insightful and surprisingly well read. His favorite book was Crash by J.G. Ballard, I was fascinated with Gravity's Rainbow by Thomas Pynchon.

Alfredo wasn't a partier or a drinker so on the nights that I wasn't working Alfredo became my frequent companion on my late-night jaunts through lower Manhattan, we would wander the city, aimlessly walking, talking about everything and nothing at all until the wee hours of the morning.

Alfredo dragged to me to Coney Island to introduce me to his family on one occasion

Alfredo, as time went on, increasingly gravitated to the art scene. He had started hanging out at galleries, then doing part time work hanging shows or just generally helping out at Fun Gallery and 56 Wooster Gallery then gradually transitioned into him assisting artists directly as he got to know people in the art scene.

First working for David Art Wales, the Australian artist best known for creating the satirical cult figure Guru Adrian. David gave Alfredo room and board in his marvelously dilapidated one bedroom apartment on St. Marks place in exchange for help producing work.

From working and living with David Alfredo transitioned to a similar situation assisting Toby Mott and Paul Spencer of the Grey Organization, a British Art Collective notorious for their Cork Street attack in the UK. Toby and Paul took Alfredo under their wing, particularly Toby, and gave him something of a crash course in 20th century art along the way so that he could better understand the work that they were doing. In the Grey's orbit Alfredos knowledge of art and art history greatly expanded. He became fascinated with the work of Joseph Beuys and also took more than a passing interest in the work of Gilbert & George the notable British Art collective and collective art in general. He and I, at his insistence, even formed our own short-lived art collective, the aptly named "Knights of Idleness" But making and selling our own art was not really going to put food on the table and we had had some success acting as middlemen for art deals.

Alfredo started to seek out out artists and gallerists as friends. Through the Grey's he got to know Ben Buchanan, the downtown nightlife photographer and personal assistant to Eric Goode the nightclub impresario, he cultivated friendships with art critics, writers and curators such as René Ricard, Anthony Haden-Guest and Kenny Schachter. He got to know gallerists such as Papo Calo of Exit Art, and of course continued to foster his relationship with Ronald Sosinski of Donahue Gallery/the Proposition who would become so important to his later professional art career.

In 1989 the markets had just taken a rather dramatic downturn due to the crash of the Junk Bond market and people who had been buying art as a hobby now found that they would appreciate a way to very quietly take their 2nd and 3rd rate impressionists and lesser modern masters and turn them back into capital without anyone noticing that they might be strapped for cash at the moment. Brokering these deals was lucrative and quick and we managed to make a fair bit of money doing so in a short period of time. Having money in my pockets from these deals I stepped away from working for my family and became Alfredo's full-time partner in art dealing. to keep expenses down we become roommates, taking a two-bedroom corner apartment in the newly opened Red Square on Houston St. in NYC's Lower East Side.

The apartment was stark and minimal in its design with "Safe" a painting by Graham Gilmore on the entry wall, one over-designed chair against the partition wall between the kitchen and the living room, large throw pillows strewn about the floor instead of a sofa. The single largest piece of "furniture" in the apartment was eight foot long live-edge slab of wood supported on cinderblocks upon which we placed a television, stereo amp, cassette player and turntable. The only other objects to be seen were a few completed Japanese Gundam model kits placed in odd corners for a splash of color (these were the basis for Alfredos giant robot sculptures) and a couple of small halogen lamps which we made from broken cinderblocks and rusted wire lath.

While we were in Red Square Alfredo's thoughts and fascination was turning towards weapons, not guns specifically, not yet, but weapons. He became fascinated with converting everyday objects into weapons as would be done by prisoners in prison, which he did in his spare time when I wasn't around the house. I would come home after a day out to find he had taken innocuous household objects such as the toothbrushes and melted the bristles into one solid mass which he then honed and sharpen that to a razors edge (He neglected to mention

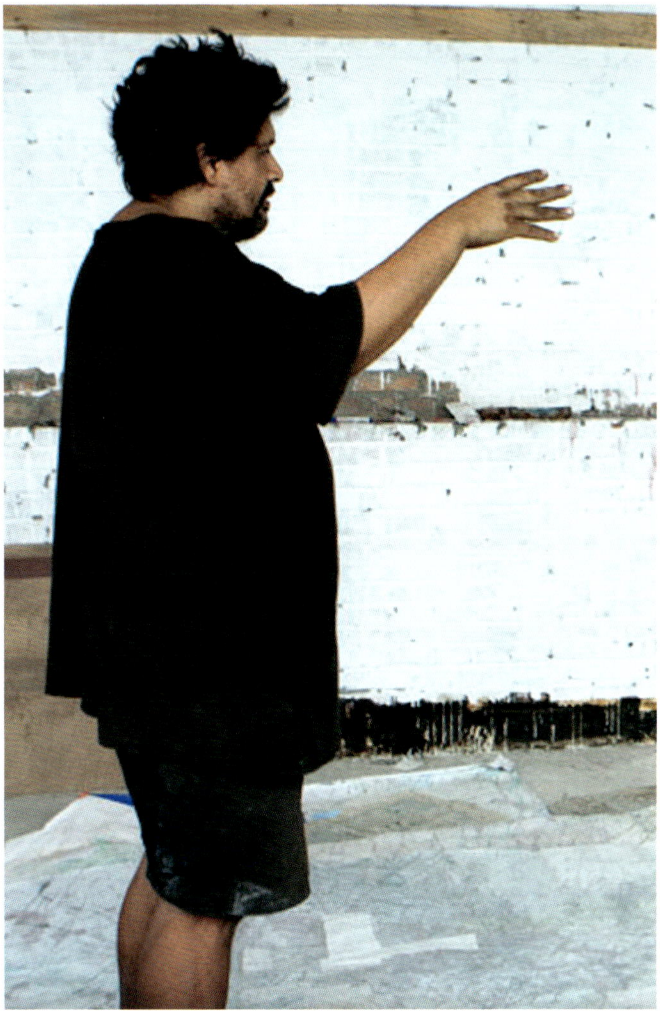

that he had taken my toothbrush to perform this experiment). Plastic Cafe Bustelo lids were melted down and turned into makeshift knives (After a few lidless days I transferred the coffee into a Mason Jar), zip guns made from office supplies, turning rubber bands, pens, and paperclips into functional single use pistols. Alfredo was very excited about this stuff and would talk me through the processes of how he was making it when we sat down together at the end of the day. I did not really realize it then, but this was Alfredo's first body of artworks made entirely in his own right.

Living and working together we lived out of each other's pockets. We never did anything more than rudimentary accounting, running a mental tally of how much came in, how much we spent and how much was left over. Money came in, Money went out, and then, all at once the money stopped flowing and we were broke. Neither of us had a job or any other financial resources, ultimately forcing us to give up the apartment and go our separate ways.

Jonathan Goldstein is a retired recording business consultant and armchair design historian.

FORE

ALFREDO MARTINEZ (1974-1999) by CHRIS KELLY

Like made to order. This art can kill you. Serious. Put that in your electric chair Andy. Guernicize it all you like. This shits for real.

See Martinez will no Longer ·pretend. The Artists now need to step up. Mondrian done did yours in. How Flat thecanvas, how absurd. But Now what?

Take Fredo's pencil drawings. The ones with the garnish of red ink. Portraits of guns, with details on the side, firing pin, shit like That, Technical sort of Thing. And across the computer paper (upon which the shit is drawn) Thick, Brown, Red, Rottingartist's arsenal.

A Martinez .45 stares you right in The Face. Barrell between the eyes. You're scared. It could be loaded. You saw This Mother Fucker on M.T.V., he's crazy. Now you stand with John's target right in front of your Face. Or a deathly Schiele, or the Mummy of an Egyptian king 2,000 years dead, Scared? No. Maybe impressed. But what could scare us, Viet-Nam Been Like, before we was born. Death everyday in the CNN. Motherfuckers be gettin thrown off bridges and shit. But a gun in your face? Loaded? probably not. Maybe. This cat don't play. I done told you that. You better see for yourself. Get that Martinez gun between your teeth. Chew upon that shit. ?Memling? Feel the potential, pulling the fucking; the fucking trigger till it goes click. Bang. You're Dead.

hues stain the sheet. It's Blood.Blood of the artist, no need to sign it, what with DNA tests and all. Grim blood from the infected toenail of the artist. Gruenewald wished he lived in such an age as this, or at least he would have, had he known. Art is over now, enter the real, Fuck your snow shovels,and "urinals", your "Brillo Boxes" and "Savarin Cans", This is real.

And we hang it on our walls because it is real. It is real suffering, It is real pain. It is real violence. It is not a representation of a gun, but the reality of the gun's violence. Splayedbeforethe club kids paying their dues, Free booze, and a gander at the next one. 70's 60's and all everybodys shakin they heads. "It's like the fucking stock market", barks Martinez it's usefull when the shit goes down."

Ane Neath the Baechlor's and Arcadia's; Fredo would roll, to and fro, fucking back and forth. Sucking it all in: Painfull, Real, Horrid, Solid, Terrible, Actual, Memeory. Aion and Chonos in the everinstant.

This is the stark reality of Martinez. Thanx to the bad. You cannot hide. No soft folds, no linear fuckin perspective to walk into, or onto. His work is about your death and mine. Great fears? But the only way to escape our fears is to confirm them. Nothing becomes something in the trappings of his Atheist Iconography.

WORD

Back to Duchamp, indulge me, in his work, Jest, laugh at the state we're in. why. you don't even know what Art is. Neither do I. What the fuck. ok. Let's see.

Back to Martinez. Art is a cop's gun. Yeah, he'll show you his art. Grab it. There it is, you want it. Take it. It's 2 a.m. in the Astor Place Station. Cop stands next to you. Grab his gun. There it is; Take it; it's perfect. But then of course you would be shot. die. shot to death, trying to take the cop's gun.

And that, is the Martinez hook. Take it. But it's dangerous. It's Like Joycean sexuality in the 30's, Like Black Pantherism in the 60's. The Nineties belong to Martinez.

Art that can kill. ?Tired of the art your 5 year old could have produced? Your 5 year old makes a fucking Martinez piece and you better raise her allowance. Cause This piece is a piece, we're talking lazar sight and silencer.

Perhaps the canvas has found its grave. Next to the easel paintings, across from the Impress(express)ionists. Maybe our world has been reduced to function, hope it is; big as Life: Motorcycles and planes, cable TV, E-mail and allthe rest of our modern Marvels. Man, those toys all work, kids don't want toy soldiers, they want military video games. So don't give us a picture of war (always inadequate), give us the tools, give us reality. It's fucking T.V.. Us/You. Do you hear me?... Painters?. Sculpters?. You've never been challenged like this. Straight up in your face. Give us reality. Make your art work. With gears and shifts and programs and cells and chips and whatever the fuck it takes. Cause the world is running past us. We are a dying breed. Martinez points ahead. We dread to look but must. we long for the old days, but love our MTV, what happened to aesthetics? while we count our twenties ever so carefully. $500 in Philly, $2,000 in N.Y.C.

But Fredo won't Let shit slide. Bang, you're dead. Your art, like the cop's gun, Forbidden by law, unauthorized, leads us to the pointof refusal. Will you break the Law? will you own a Martinez? will you hang on your wall war reality? I swear it is the only weapon left. Dig it Baby. Mind this shit, because the dawn is just begining to come.

One time Fredo told me he'd Like to lay in a tank full of water, in a gallery. For 1 month. He said, "It would have pedals inside, attached to tank treds on the outside that would carry it 1 inch per hour." He would pedal himself to and fro along the long walls, through the phat middle spaces of the Elite Downtown Galleries. Through the corridors of the New Art with the fucking Soho scene, with... … … … …

Chris Kelly was lost to a tragic accident in May, 1999, in New York City before completing this essay.

FORAGING WITH THE OF AL

by Ronald Sosinski

Having had a public Gallery in NYC for over 30 years, I have represented and have had endless encounters with so many artists, but none have equaled the intensity of Alfredo Martinez. Also, as director of the gallery and an obsessive collector, I have accumulated hundreds of artworks which are lovingly tucked away in our storage in Chelsea. While attempting to catalogue this enormous collection I came upon a treasure load of works by Alfredo Martinez. This became the basis for this book, covering the period during which I represented and was the only gallery to exhibit Martinez's work in a formal gallery setting. I had two major shows: "Who Dares Wins" in 1999 curated by Kenny Schachter and the works from prison "The United Sates of America VS. Alfredo Martinez" in 2003 curated by James Fuentes.

While sorting through the stored and mostly forgotten cache, I was startled to find almost the entirety of the exhibited works from both shows along with multiple other series which were produced for various art fairs at that time. Along with these extraordinary works I also uncovered files of reviews and other writing relating to this time period and Martinez's activities. These are the contents of this book devoted to re-claiming a place in art history for this artist forever known as the "fake Basquiat" maker. The works speak for themselves as highly unique compositions made under the most difficult of circumstances. The works and the accompanying press will be complimented by various essays. Jonathan Jay Goldstein, the official biographer of Martinez, through his extensive research, has created the definitive bio and early NYC history of the artist in the Introduction. The Forward will be replaced by a poetic/punk essay composed by the young curator Chris Kelly written in 1999 while working with Alfredo but left unfinished because of his untimely death.

James Fuentes now a well-known and successful gallery owner in NYC and LA has agreed to allow me to re-publish the ex-

FOR GOLD GHOST FREDO

traordinary essay/interview "Why you fuckin' with my boy Picasso?" The Saga of Alfredo Martinez continues..." which he did with Alfredo while in prison. He was the official curator chosen by Alfredo in 2003 for the "The United States of America VS.Alfredo Martinez" Drawings from Prison show at The Proposition.

James is also responsible for the great title of the show which will also be the title of the book on Alfredo. Many thanks.An incredible super essay by Marc Hungerbuhler will trace his personal relationship with Martinez from the formative years of his development through an exciting and challenging time they spent in China as curators and artists. This is extremely insightful into the personality and internal engine propelling Martinez.

At this point, since Martinez, artist and curator, will be forever remembered for his "fake Basquiat "I would like to drop an artworld anecdote about Pontus Hulten. Hulten, director of the Moderna Museet, Stockholm, gave Andy Warhol his first solo museum exhibition in 1968.In 2007 it was discovered that Hulten had commissioned 105 Warhol Brillo Boxes in 1990, three years after the artist's death, for an exhibition in St. Petersburgh. These "fakes" were bought by many reputable dealers unsuspectingly. This action now taints? Hulten's reputation but provoked the Stockholm Museum to question about what can be regarded as original and a copy in art. Hulten died in 2006 a year before the discovery. Caravaggio (1571-1610) spent his entire life running from the law, proving that all great art transcends the maker. A bonus essay by Tom Jarmusch will delve into the generosity of Martinez to other artists and his valuable place as a curator during this period in the NYC art world. A final thank you to Terrence Sanders Smith of Artvoices Books for his trust and bold choice to publish and bring this material and artist forward at this crucial time in our cultural history.

THE UNITED STATES VS ALFREDO MARTINEZ

Alfredo Martinez convinced an art collector to purchase two drawings by Jean-Michel Basquiat (which belonged to Tom Warren) in the late winter of 2001 for a bargain price. The work in question appeared that December in an exhibition Martinez co-curated with James Fuentes entitled, “Welcome to the Playground of the Fearless”. Martinez took charge of returning the pieces to Warren, but before doing so, made his own versions. After returning the drawings, he mentioned that there was interest in the work from collectors who saw the show. He said he wanted to make copies of the certificates of authenticity before shopping the work around. Warren handed over the certificates, which Martinez went on to forge as well, he then returned falsified certificates and sold fake paintings” with real certificates” to the collector. The collector was tipped off that the paintings were fake by a Chelsea dealer and subsequently notified the F.B.I.

THE UNITED STATES VS ALFREDO MARTINEZ

Claiming to be collectors the F.B.I. led Martinez to make more Basquiat drawings and certificates in an elaborate sting operation. His later forgeries were apparently sloppy compared to the first ones, as a result of his carelessness & and a possible desire to get caught (not to mention the encouragement from the F.B.I. for him to make more), he was apprehended by the F.B.I. on June 19, 2002. Forgery is difficult to prove however, so during the sting, the undercover F.B.I. agent posing as a collector named Bob Clay, asked Alfredo to Fed Ex and email a photo of the works in question across state lines. Federal prosecutors found him guilty on four counts of mail fraud and one count of wire fraud which led to a mandatory sentencing of at least three years of jail. He currently resides at the Metropolitan detention Center in Brooklyn, three blocks away from where Martinez grew up.

THE UNITED STATES VS ALFREDO MARTINEZ

THE UNITED STATES VS ALFREDO MARTINEZ

Alfredo Martinez' art career began in 1993 at Pat Heam Gallery, the show was a happening called "Skater Angels" produced by David Greenberg and Diego Cortez. Afterwards he went on to participate in the seminal "Bong Show" at Alleged Gallery where artists such as Tom Sachs and Dirk Westphal made elaborate bongs as sculpture. His heights of legitimacy came first when he exhibited in group shows at the P.S. 1 Museum, a MoMa Affiliate ("Agent Artist", "Generation Z"), that same year he had his first career solo show at the Donahue Sosinski gallery in SoHo (this exhibition marks his second solo exhibit with the gallery). In the summer of 2000 Roberta Smith reviewed an exhibition he curated "Na' er Do Wells" for The New York Times.

THE UNITED STATES VS ALFREDO MARTINEZ

That same year, a dot-com millionaire Joshua Harris (in collaboration with Leo Koenig) financed an indoor firing range designed by Martinez for a millennial project entitled "Quiet". These were noteworthy achievements for someone who never graduated high school. In a field where academic legitimacy is highly revered (in most cases required), Martinez managed to do remarkably well with only an eleventh-grade education. In this regard, he is a true folk artist, an elitist term synonymous with "outsider", a derelict. During his time in federal prison, he continues to make art. This is significant because despite all of his escapades, his primary interest is still in making a career for himself as an artist. Were his actions just a desperate attempt to earn a quick buck? A decisive critique of the sometimes-absurd values we place on art objects? Or is he in jail on purpose?

THE UNITED STATES VS ALFREDO MARTINEZ

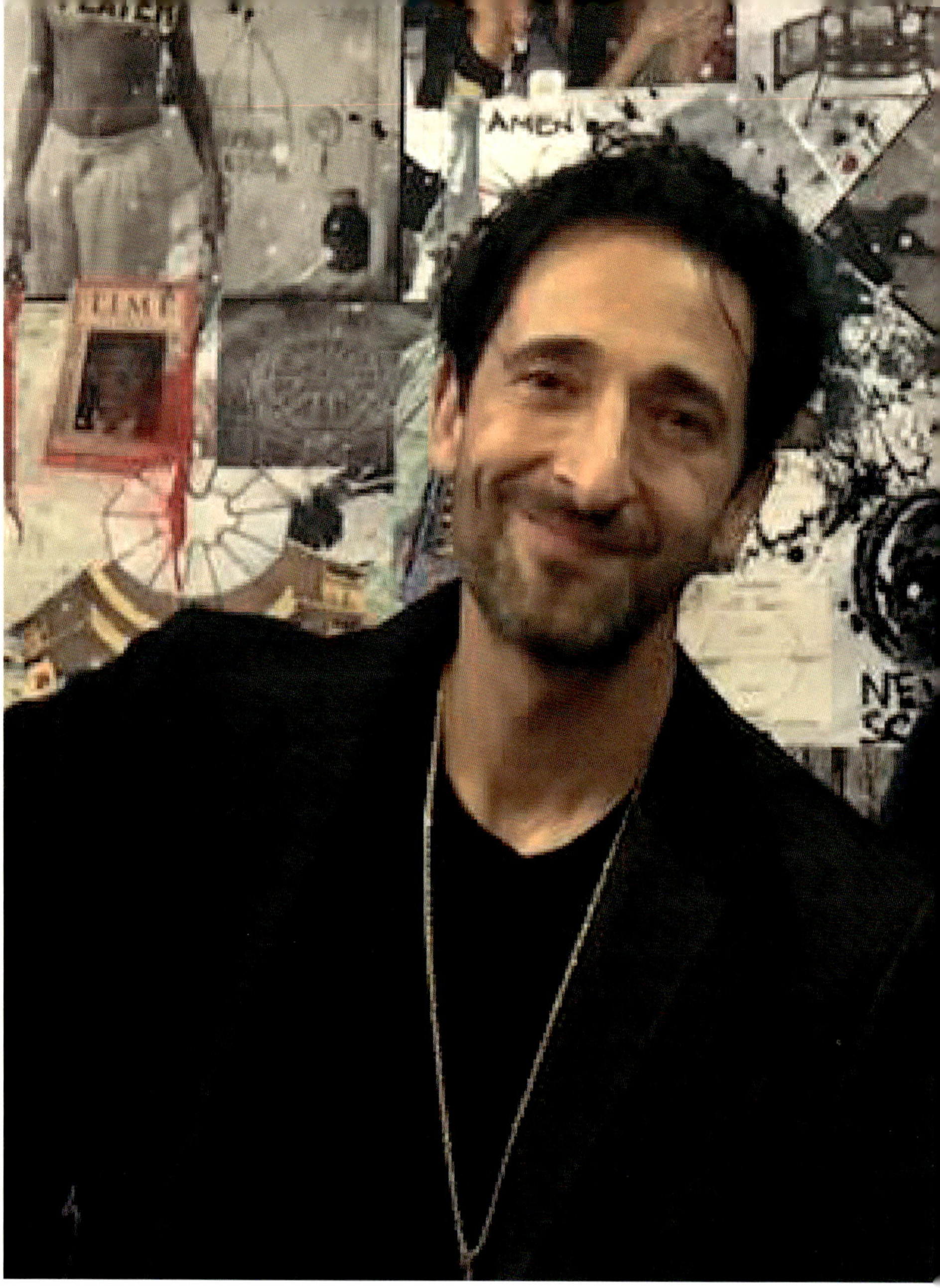

Adrien Brody and Alfredo Martinez.
Photo by Julia Morrison

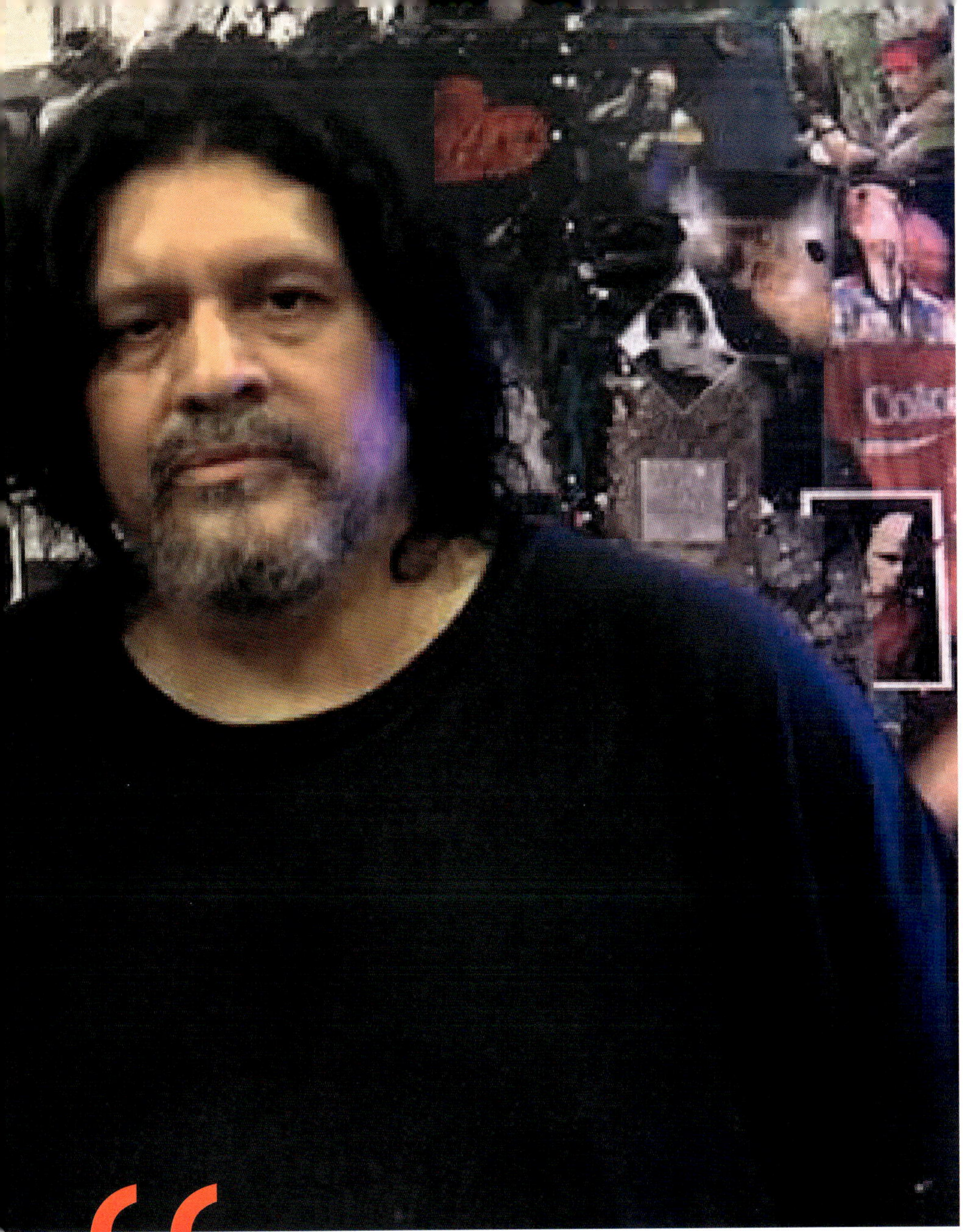

"

Alfredo Martinez was larger than life, an inspiration and a friend who always tried to help me along my path as an artist, He spotted me through the widow of my storefront studio on the Bowery back in 2016 and came in "guns blazing," armed with stories and brandishing an arsenal of colorful gun paintings that I was so enamored with, I bought them on the spot. He shared tales of hardship and triumph, he was an original who was also notorious for forging Basquiat, eventually landing him in Rikers. Alfredo passed away last Sunday night. I'm grateful to have known him. He will be missed. Rest In Peace my friend.

Adrien Brody

2 Time Academy Award Winning Actor

Designed by Christa Phoebe Gilna

ISBN: 979-8-9912234-5-4
Library of Congress Control Number: 2026936462
Printed in China

Published by Artvoices Art Books a division of Artvoices Books

ARTVOICES BOOKS
www.artvoicesbooks.com

THE UNITED STATES VS ALFREDO MARTINEZ

Ronald Sosinski

ARTVOICES BOOKS

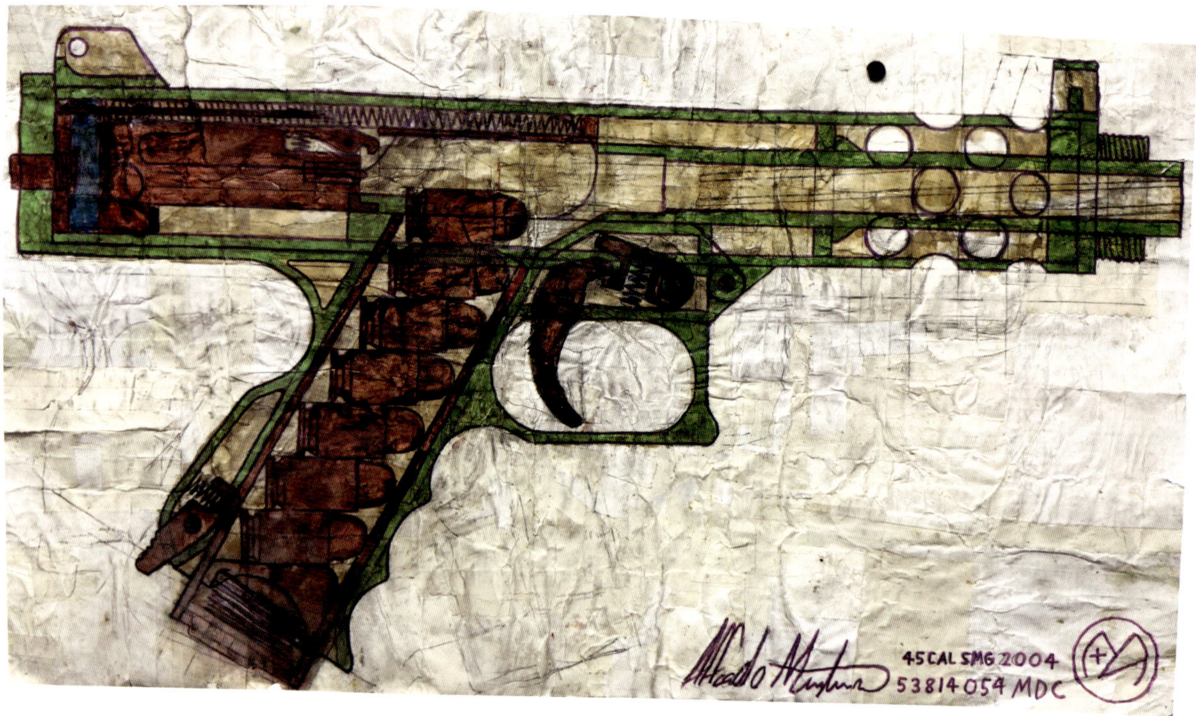

Gun Drawing #1

2004

Mixed Media on Hand Collaged Paper

18 x 28.5 in.

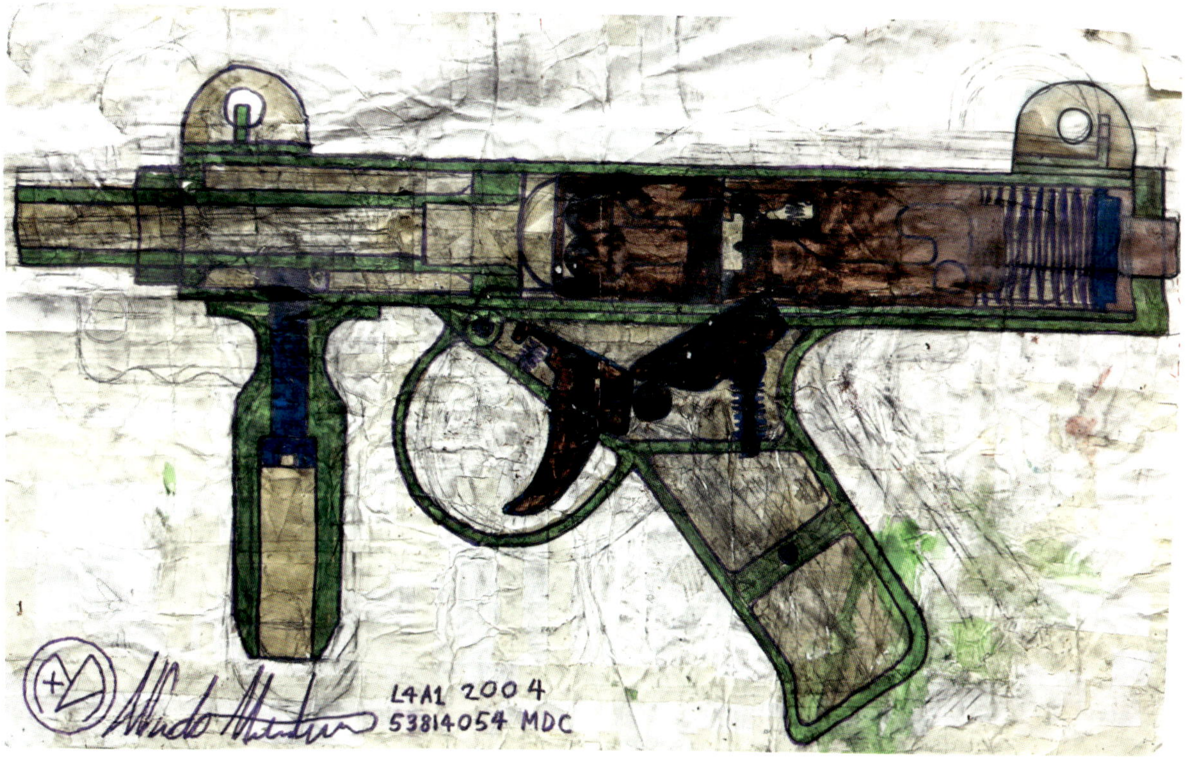

Gun Drawing #2

2004

Mixed Media on Hand Collaged Paper

18 x 28.5 in.

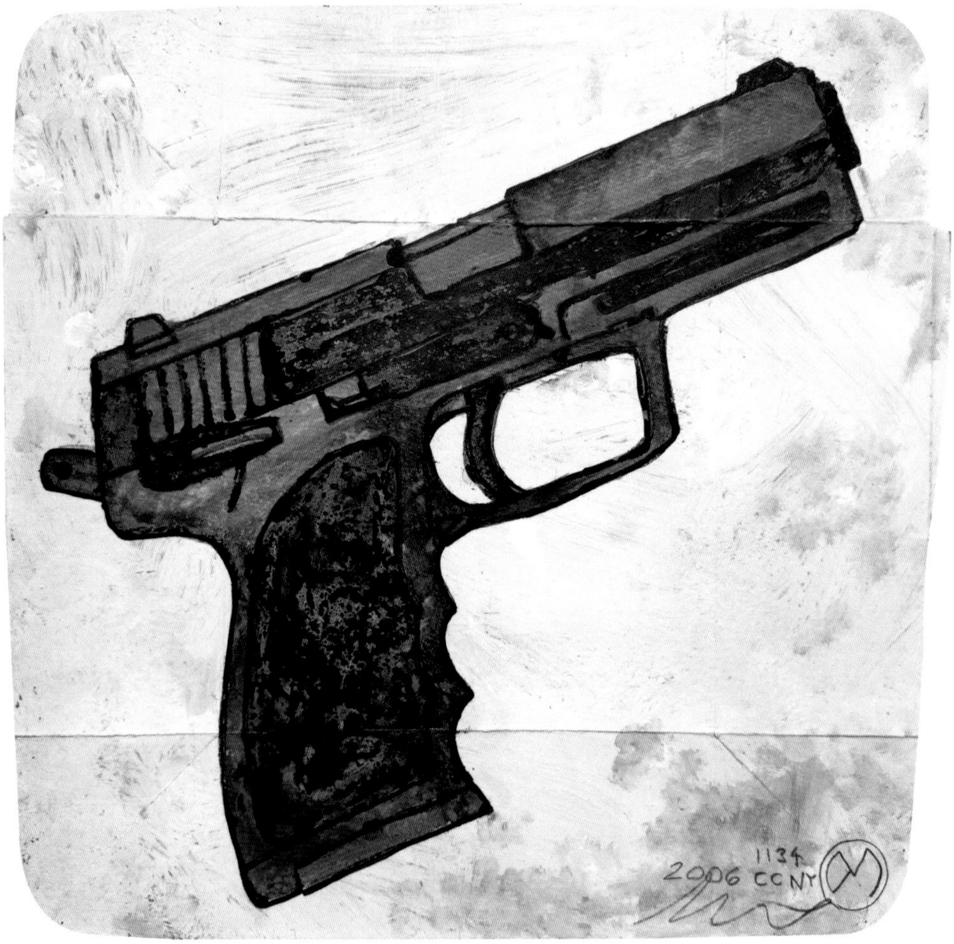

Single Gun

2006

Mixed Media on Hand Collaged Paper

22 x 22 in.

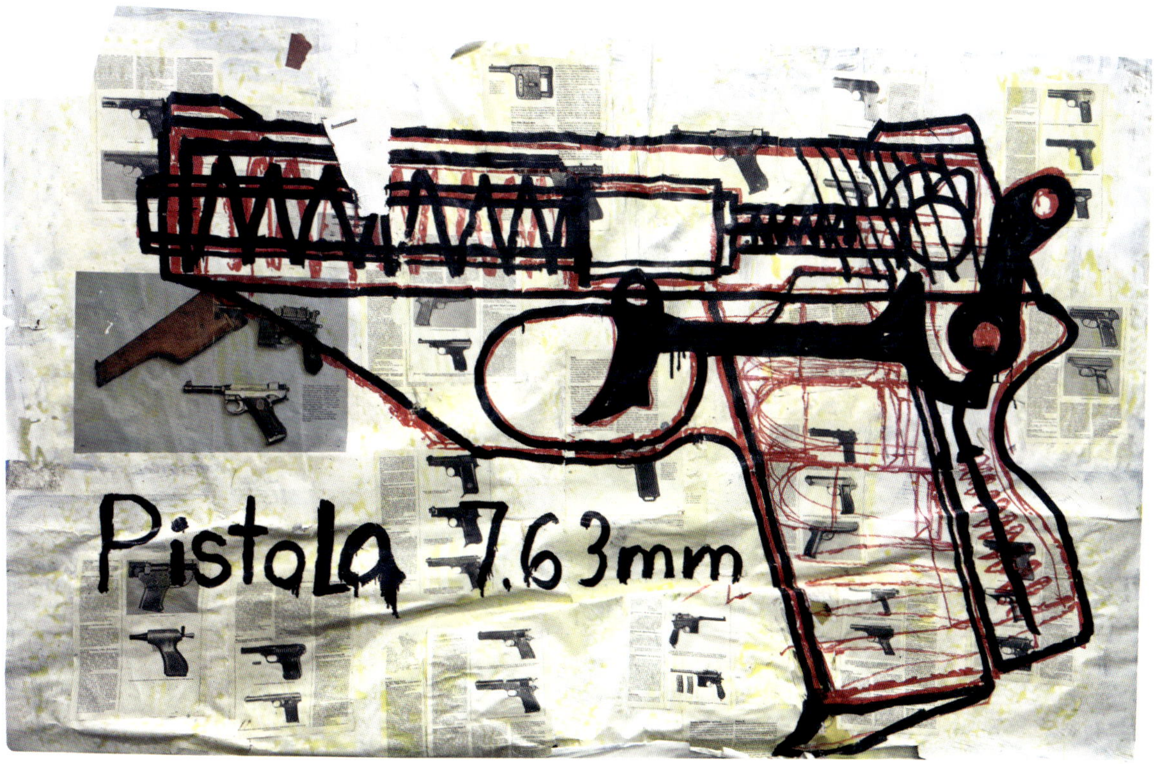

Pistola

1999

Mixed Media on Hand Collaged Paper

56 x 90 in.

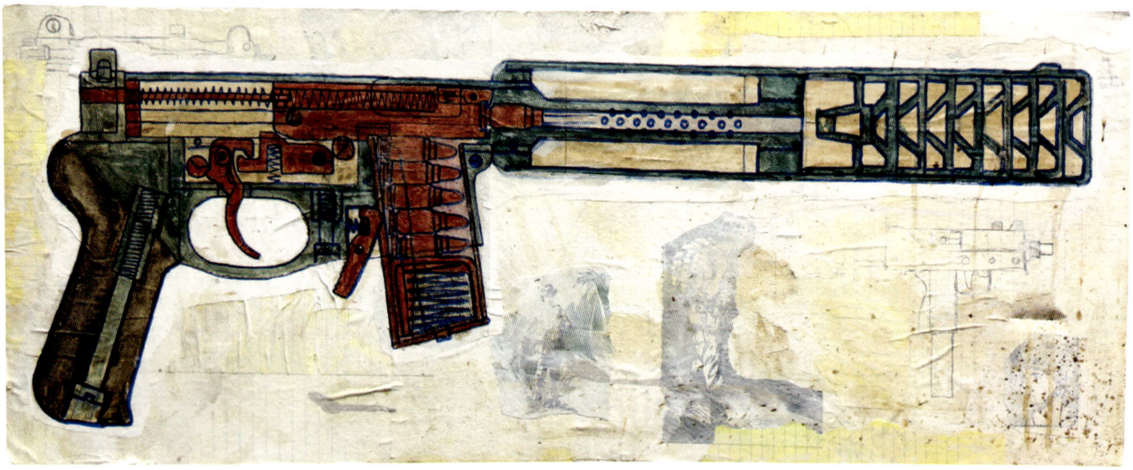

Gun Drawing #3

1999

Mixed Media on Canvas

30 c 12 x 2.5 in.

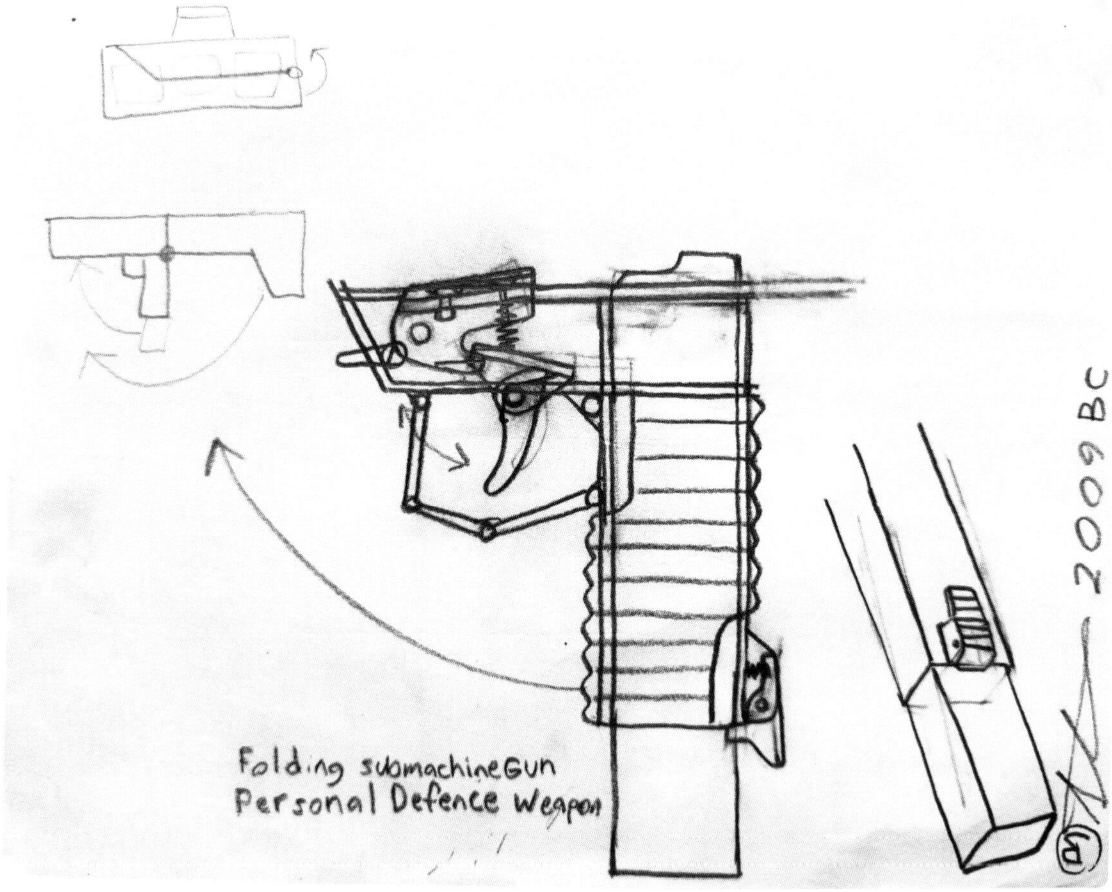

Notebook Drawing #1

2009

Mixed Media on Hand Collaged Paper

11 x 14 in.

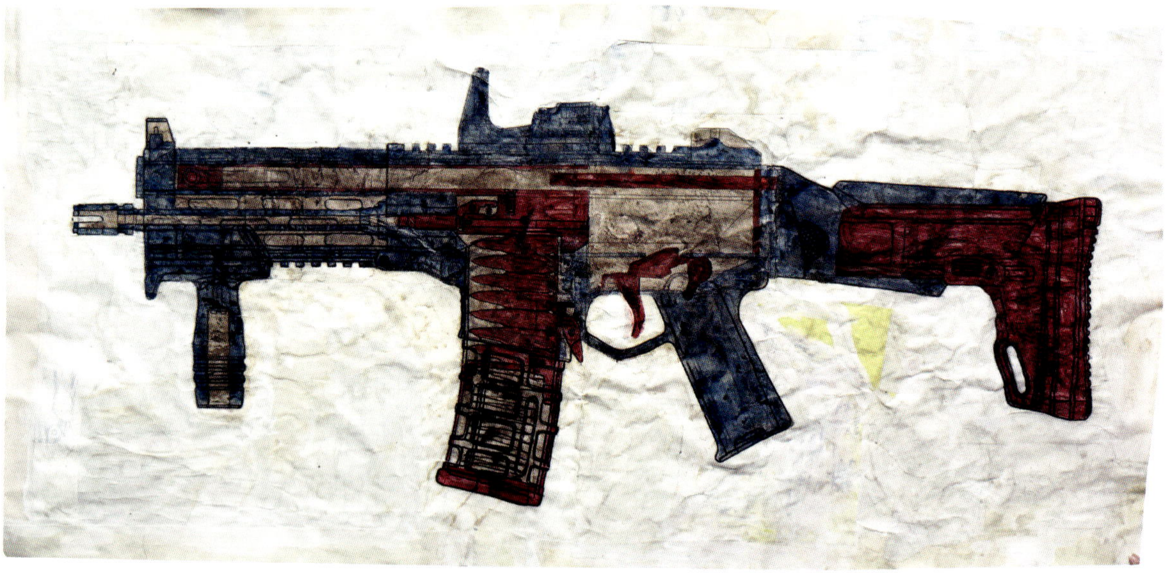

Gun Drawing #4

1999

Mixed Media on Hand Collaged Paper

30 x 64 in.

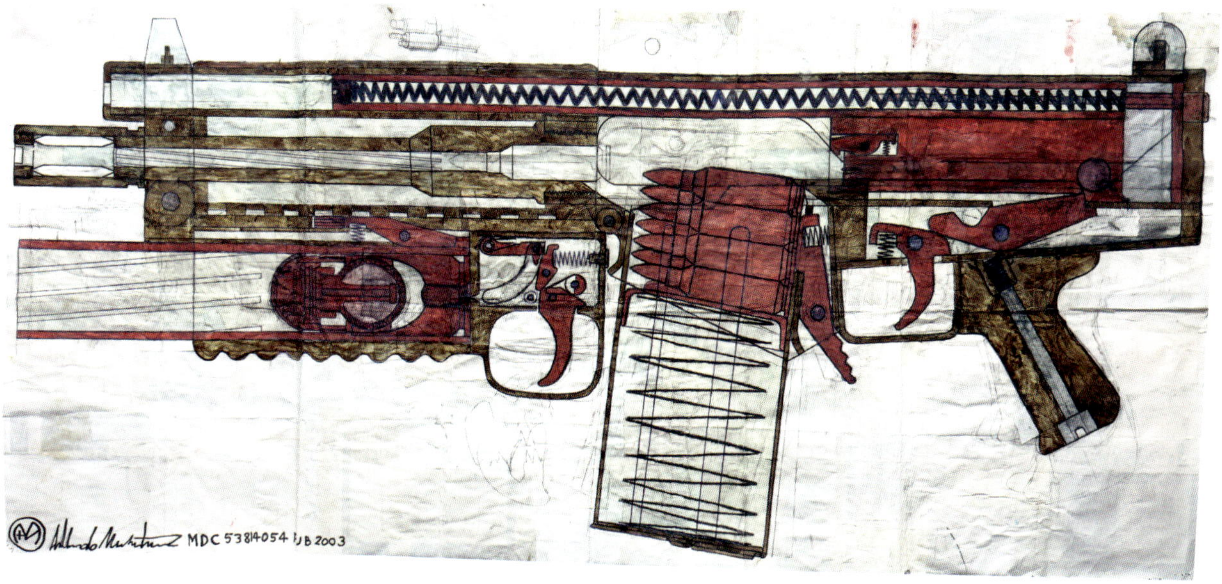

Gun Drawing #5

2003

Mixed Media on Hand Collaged Paper

32 x 71 in.

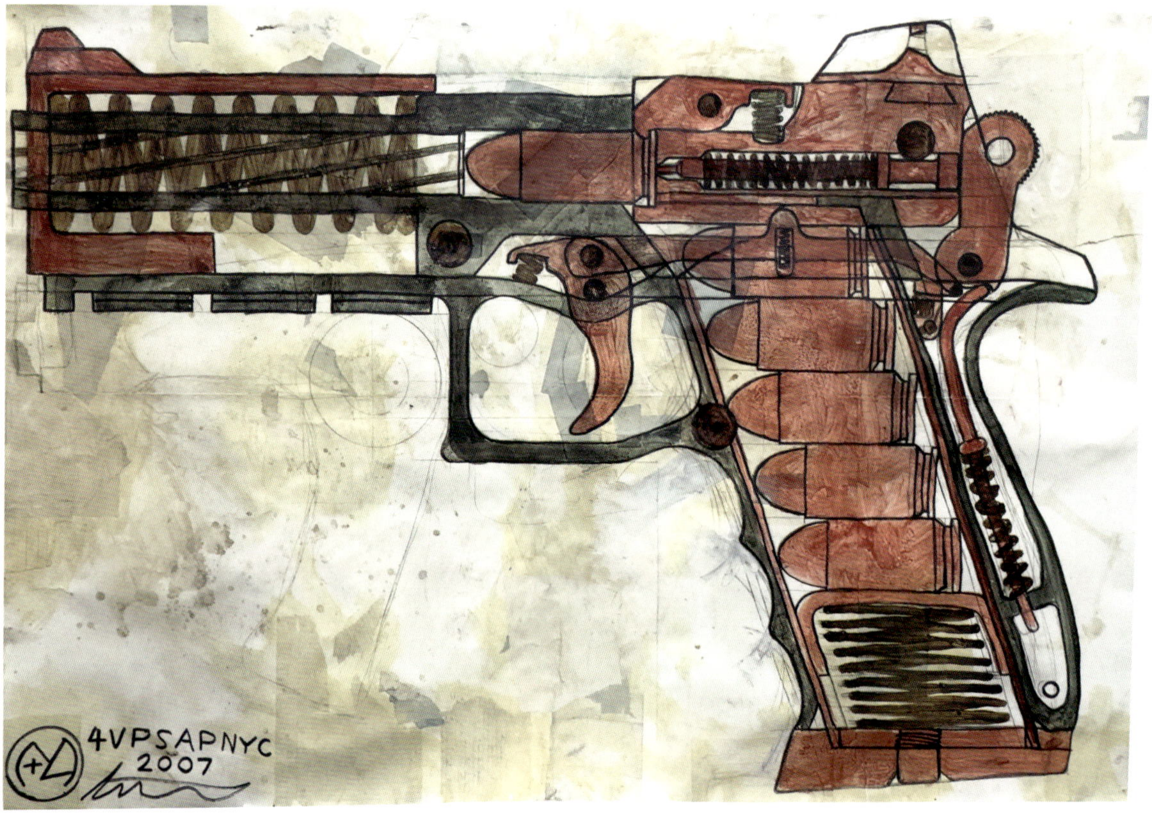

Gun Drawing #6

2007

Mixed Media on Hand Collaged Paper

18 x 32 in.

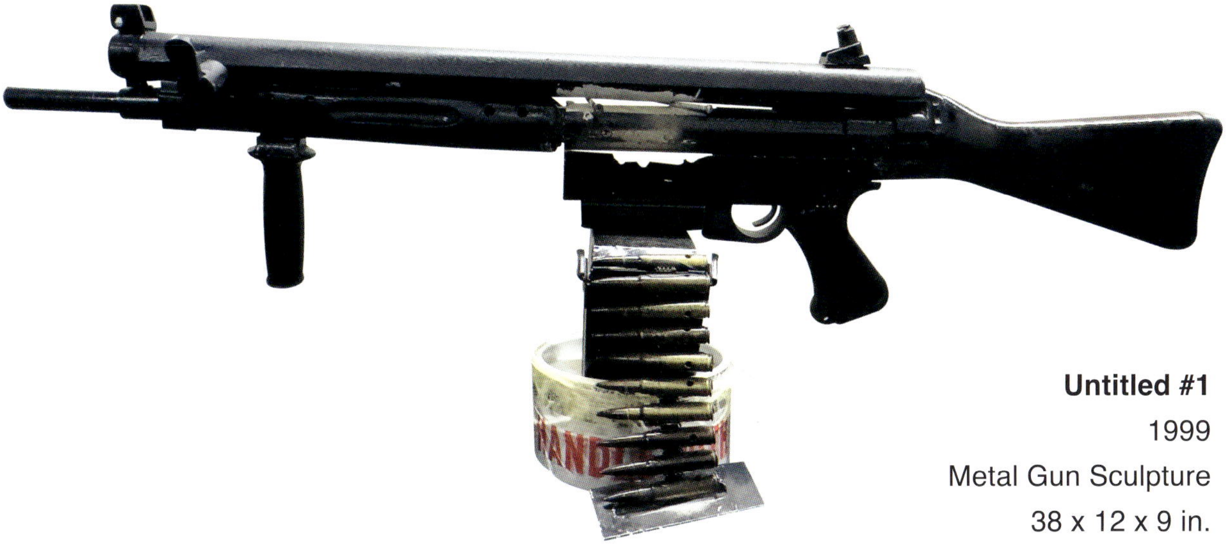

Untitled #1
1999
Metal Gun Sculpture
38 x 12 x 9 in.

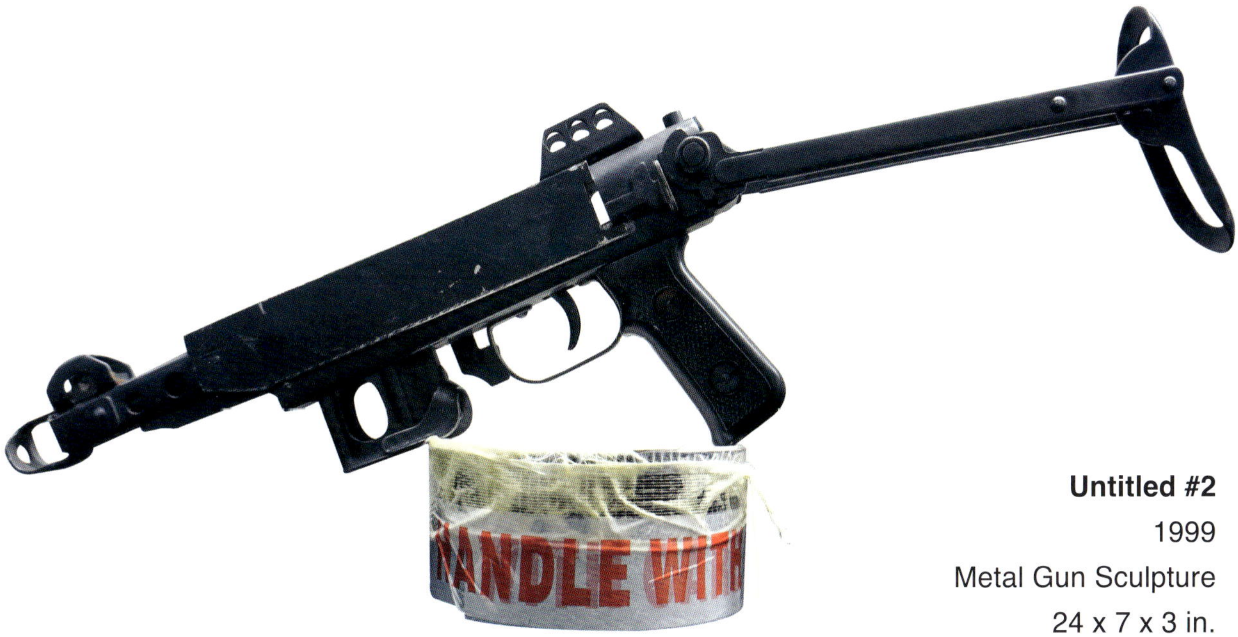

Untitled #2
1999
Metal Gun Sculpture
24 x 7 x 3 in.

ALFRED

by Tom Jarmusch

I met Alfredo during pre-production of Ghost Dog: The Way Of The Samurai, my brother Jim's movie. I was taping together location photos at night in a nondescript Chelsea office. Alfredo walks by with another man close behind. With a sweet voice Alfredo says, “Hi Tom.” “Hi Alfredo” I reply. Minutes later I realized the man with him was Ghost Dog, Forrest Whitaker in character and in costume. I had just thought he was some friend of Alfredo's. Alfredo worked for the film as a weapons and props consultant, and with Forrest how to handle these homemade looking guns. I think this job didn't last long after production got an invoice from Alfredo. Prior to this Alfredo and I had met in the hallway having a friendly casual conversation. Jim hadn't known Alfredo long either.

This would be our pattern almost until Alfredo died. Alfredo would appear, often excited with wild ideas, a show he was working on and he wanted me in. At this time, I made a lot of photos, and small films and videos often spontaneous and not finished. The first show I was in with and for Alfredo was in 1999, something he curates with James Tully. Weeks before Alfredo came over to my apartment and looked at photos all over my bed and boxes around. He wanted to show lots as they were unframed, and told me, encouraged me to make some drawings, which I didn't really do. I made some 9x14 kids' newsprint and black marker. I liked the drawings. The show was in a large two floor odd commercial space in the garment district. We got the show installed and had a big opening. Upstairs across from my wall was M. Henry Jones with a large moving animated sculpture. Also in the show were

O & ME

Matt and Mark Enger, and Alfredo and James. I'm not sure now who else. The following day we were all locked out and our work locked in. The locks had been changed. I'm not sure how Alfredo and James had keys. After days we got our work out. Later Alfredo was involved with Josh Harris and his project show QUIET in an entire rented building on lower Broadway near Franklin. I wasn't directly in the show, I wasn't into the surveillance idea of Josh's, or podland and artists in jumpsuits living on site. Alfredo designed and had a shooting gallery built with large windows viewers could look in. I was able to hook up Alfredo with a theatrical weapons specialist, rentals etc. This allowed Alfredo access for any gun he imagined, some crazy stuff like Al Capone used. The on-site specialists made all the weapons and blanks legal. I also was able to get a NYC movie shoot permit for Josh. A permit was not necessary for any filming or video that would be inside. There was a lot of videos being shot by Ondi Timor and others. The Mayor's Office of Film and TV was like you don't need permits. I insisted typing on the form in the city office, "Request permission for camera on sticks (tripod) on the sidewalk in front of (whatever address on Broadway) will not obstruct pedestrian traffic." I was paid quite well by Josh for the shooting permit and weapons specialists' contact. I used my money to buy black and white 16mm film and used my Bolex to film Alfredo with guns and hanging out. This was hard to do because people were invited in to learn how to shoot while others looked in the windows. It seemed more often than not the room was full of beautiful girls. The room was a non-stop performance. I wanted to film Alfredo alone. On New Years Eve night Millenium 2000 QUIET was raided and closed by FEMA and the NY Fire Department. Apparently, they thought QUIET was possibly a millennial death cult. The movie permit and weapons specialists proved useful and made everything legal.

There were other shows. Alfredo would appear with some ideas and a few suggestions, turn me onto a Chinatown film lab (that I didn't know) or a 99 cents store in Chelsea. One show I had a series of photos mostly from a cheap phone and cheap prints framed crudely on black paper. I still have this work and am surprised when I see it.

Alfredo had a way of being with artists and encouraging them. Sometimes he'd get artists to begin doing kinds of work they never have done, like painting with him in whatever studio wherever he was living. I'm pretty sure he did this with more than one artist. Like he had been with me and drawings and whatever few suggestions, and maybe a little money to make whatever work. He'd set me free to do whatever I wanted. It was partly how he curated Alfredo was never a gate keeper and never controlling everything. Alfredo was an artist and a provocateur. He would set up the artists with whatever input or resources, all his various schemes to score big or whatever the plan was. Then let everything run its course. The shows always felt kinetic and lively no matter what the work and ideas were, like anything might happen at any minute. Alfredo often had some known artists and then artists he found and liked.

I think Alfredo is under appreciated, and little known as a curator and who nurtured artists. Looking back over these times working with Alfredo I really appreciate the freedom and confidence working with him. I've seldom experienced anything like this in the gallery world I've known.

I have and have had a lot of feelings for Alfredo. We've had good and bad times. I have a big regret, unfinished work together and with some others. I owe Alfredo a very big apology.

My writing here is also a huge thank you for fun and freedom to make whatever I wanted when we worked together. This continues for me; I wish we could do another show together. And another crazy extravagant meal with lots of sushi.

Thank You Alfredo!!

Tom Jarmusch is an artist, filmmaker. He lives and works in NYC.

Time Out New York Issue 217
November 18–25, 1999

Alfredo Martinez, "Who Dares, Wins"

Donahue/Sosinski Art, through Sat 20 (see Soho).

Although Mary Boone spent a night in jail for exhibiting Tom Sachs's working shotguns, the folks at Donahue/Sosinski needn't fear a trip to the clinker. True, their current offering, a show of sculpture and drawings by Alfredo Martinez, curated by Kenny Schachter, involves guns, but they're held together with black tape. Martinez knows his firearms and could have easily made these work. But he's not into making radical-chic gestures; consequently, none of the weapons on view are functional.

Instead, it is the makeshift nature of the pieces that is the focus. Martinez likens what he's doing to the ingenuity that French Resistance fighters or the Vietcong displayed in arming themselves against vastly superior opponents. He has plopped a workbench with a vise into one corner of the gallery, where he works on additional "guns" while eagerly sharing his arcane knowledge of various makes and models with anyone who asks. Although Martinez's presence is more genial than menacing—rather like a friendly bicycle repairman's—his rap reminds me of Peter Fend, that conceptualist Jeremiah known for his ecological proselytizing. Like Fend, Martinez reaches through the bubble separating art from life—which is what makes his work so intriguing.

In the context of Martinez's residency, his four large "Gun Collages" come across as messy manifestos wallpapering an occupied zone. By themselves, they aren't much—just Donald Baechler–like outlines of guns or gun parts on large, loose canvases layered with pages from Italian or German gun manuals. Yet with Martinez in the room, they make a bold, simple statement about the iconic nature of guns. Martinez won me over with his gargantuan robots at the "Generation Z" show at P.S. 1 last year; with "Who Dares, Wins" he does it again.—*Robert Mahoney*

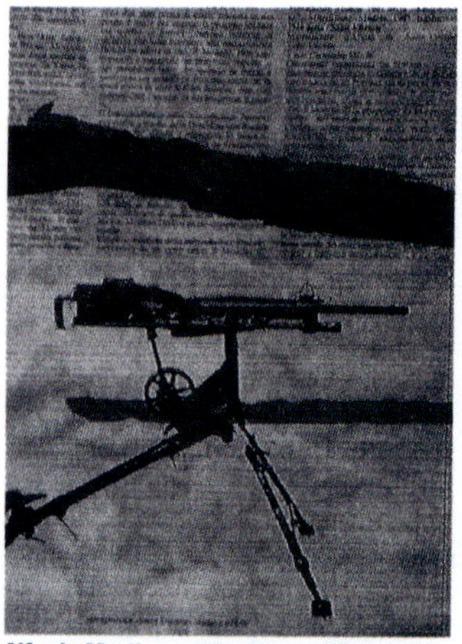

COURTESY OF DONAHUE/SOSINSKI ART

Alfredo Martinez, *Who Dares, Wins*, 1999.

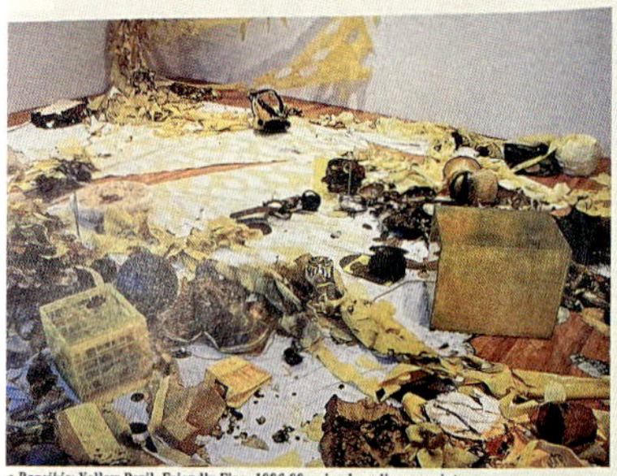

s Bareikis: Yellow Peril, Friendly Fire, *1996-99, mixed mediums, paint, erized objects and paper.*

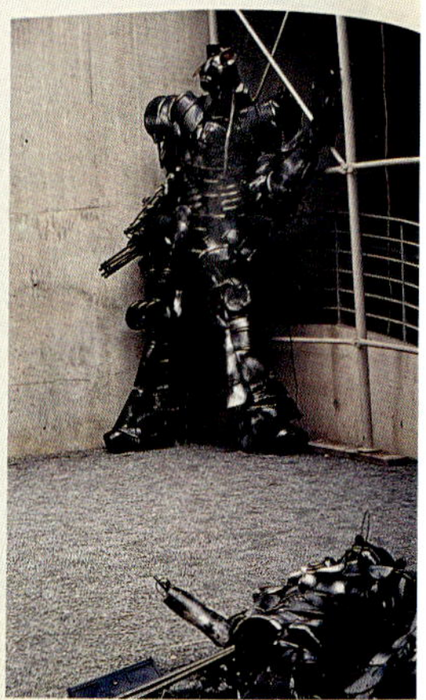

Alfredo Martinez: Andrew, *1994-99, garbage-can lids, assorted found plastic objects, spray paint. Collection Method 5.*

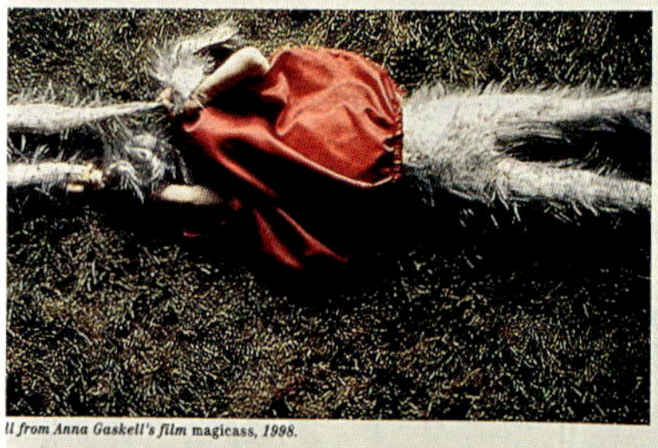

ll from Anna Gaskell's film magicass, *1998.*

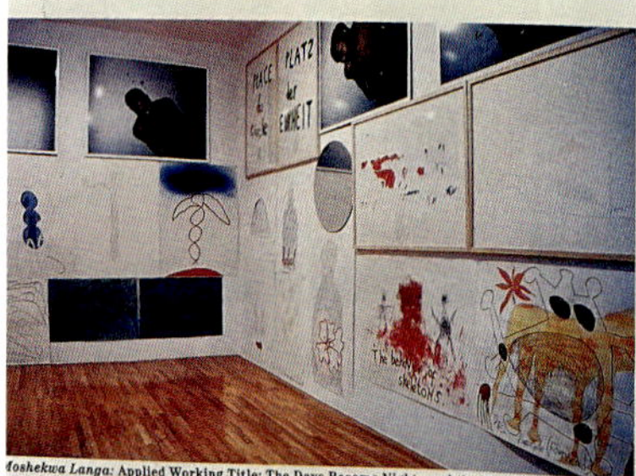

Moshekwa Langa: Applied Working Title: The Days Become Nights and the Nights Become Days, *1997-99, photographs and works on paper, dimensions variable.*

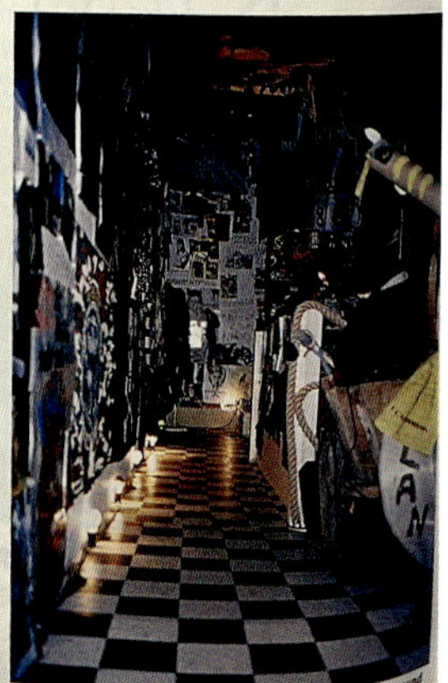

Jonathan Meese: Ahoy Angst, *1998, posters, photos, album covers, sound and video, dimensions variable. Collection Herbert Volkmann, Berlin.*

Generation Z: Slacker Than Thou

At P.S. 1, domestic debris and photographic self-portraits dominated an international exhibition of over 20 artists, almost all under the age of 35.

BY NANCY PRINCENTHAL

Organized jointly by P.S. 1's founding director Alanna Heiss, Berlin Biennale director Klaus Biesenbach (he is also a curator at P.S. 1) and Barbara Vanderlinden, a young Belgian curator, "Generation Z" was an international survey meant to be so fresh that hitting the shelves not quite ripe counts as a plus. Indeed, this assortment of work, representing more than 20 artists and collaborative groups and nearly as many countries, was billed as an "exhibition-in-progress," although plans for a second showing in Belgium eventually fell through. Beyond newness and youth (almost all the artists are under 35, and many are in their 20s), the curators pursued no particular theme. "We hope that Generation Z represents a departure from the stylish, manufactured nihilism revealed in the media's creation of a millennially-obsessed Generation X," a wall text said. But if a trend could be spotted in this show, it was a global flight from passion, manifest in an affectless introspection as insular as it is, evidently, universal.

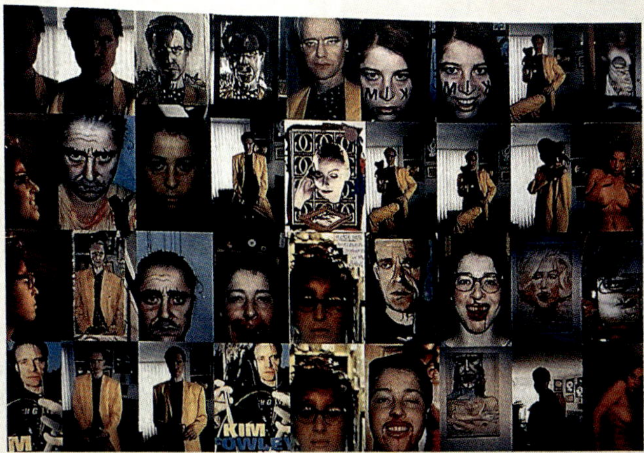

Elke Krystufek: I AM Your Mirror *(detail), 1998, framed photo-collages, each 27½ by 39⅜ inches. Photos this article courtesy P.S. 1 Contemporary Art Center, Long Island City.*

Perhaps inevitably in a show with three organizers, some juxtapositions between artists were less than felicitous—and, at the same time, revealing. This was particularly true of the many installations, by artists from places as far-flung as Bratislava and Tokyo, of barely altered or organized domestic debris. It does no service to Boris Ondreicka of Slovakia that his impenetrably messy installation, centered on a couple of worktables draped with tangled thread, shared a room at P.S. 1 with a photographic panorama of a related scene of studio mayhem by Japanese artist Tomoko Takahashi; next door was more of the same, this time in the form of color-coordinated commercial flotsam strewn on the floor by Aidas Bareikis of Vilnius. Jason Rhoades's installations, while clearly something of a paradigm, would look fastidious in comparison. Similarly, the French artist Lionel Estève's *Hello Mariano* presented accretions of tiny, flimsy things—thread, buttons, partly pulverized chalk, bags of flock, the tiny paper cups used for ketchup at fast-food restaurants—that littered floor, windowsills and walls. The piece would make Richard Tuttle's work seem formal and robust; ditto Donald Lipski's increasingly prescient-seeming *Gathering Steam* installations.

Running full-throttle along the same track, Jonathan Meese, born in Tokyo and raised in Germany, assembled a blaring, duplex rec room of memorabilia, largely in the form of news clippings and posters relating to media stars. Crudely hand-painted slogans deface pictures of the likes of Klaus Kinski, Bill Clinton, Che Guevara and Truman Capote, while at Meese's "basement" level, Stanley Kubrick's *A Clockwork Orange* played on a small video monitor, its Beethovian soundtrack providing background music.

Interspersed with the celebrity headshots were photographs of the artist, introducing a second, even more prevalent motif of "Generation Z." For all its autobiographical angst, Meese's installation was not nearly the most self-consumed in this show. Californian Brett Cook-Dizney's combination of paintings and Polaroids, childhood drawings and action figures was best at evoking the nerve-jangling world of early adolescence, but the work of Moshekwa Langa of Bakenberg, South Africa—big, slack drawings and even bigger, slacker color photographs—was pretty good, too, at suggesting the enervated anxiety of the newly grown. In the tradition (it amounts to an academy, by now) of early Cindy Sherman, Korean-born Nikki Lee took dozens of small, color photographs of herself in various guises: punk, tourist, drag queen, yuppie, lesbian, Hispanic teen. They're sharp and often funny, and seem less about cultural-construction-of-identity dogma than about the way more complicated, and basic, teenage business of trying on different looks to figure out who you are. But for prize-winning self-obsession, the hands-down winner is Elke Krystufek, a Viennese artist who here presented a whopping 1,300 photographs of herself, ranging from early adolescence to the present (she was born in 1970).

What stood out in this welter of re-created workroom dishabille and compulsive self-reflection? The fully dressed, the tight-lipped and, above all, the hard-working. Small Lucite pyramids in which vaguely menacing miniature tchotchkes are stuck as if in amber, by Vincente Razo of Mexico City; Nigerian-born Fatimah Tuggar's big, multipanel photo-collages in which tourist shots (Big Ben, Taj Mahal) segue into images of very particular real-life subsistence. Chris Sauter of Texas contributed what here counted as a conventional sculpture, an arresting work fashioned of neatly folded old clothes, bound with belts and topped with horns made of layered nylon stockings. Alfredo Martinez, a 32-year-old New Yorker described as having been a private detective, arms dealer's assistant, weapons consultant for films and, at present, part-time gunsmith, weighed in with a pair of heavy-metal gladiators, in the Mad Max tradition, that gave (misleading) showbiz drama to the exhibition's entryway. One of the better-known participants, American Anna Gaskell, created a surround-sound installation which, discreetly but disturbingly, conflated childhood and carnality in the form of a hybrid creature, half girl, half hairy goat.

These few, disparate works share no format or premise. What they have in common is credible evidence that they are intended, and even wanted, rather than seeming accidental offspring of failed ambition. Of course, diffidence is a well-defended, even entrenched, position. When first articulated, in the early '90s, it caused considerable and fruitful provocation. But, uncomfortable as it is to challenge the humble, it seems time for some questions. Is it helpful to consider whether depression (in art) can be faked? Has suspicion of mastery produced a generation of emotional malingerers? It may not be nihilism that these artists collectively convey, but it sure isn't ardent and forthright belief in art's expressive or conceptual power, either. □

"Generation Z" appeared at P.S. 1 Contemporary Art Center, New York [Apr. 18-June 6].

Author: *Nancy Princenthal is a freelance writer based in New York.*

DONAHUE / SOSINSKI ART

For Immediate Release:

"WHO DARES WINS"
Alfredo Martinez
First New York Solo Show
world premier "guns & drawings"
curated by Kenny Schachter
October 21- November 20, 1999

Opening Reception: Saturday, October 23, 6-8pm

Donahue/Sosinski Art
560 Broadway #304
New York, New York 10012

212-226-1111 fax 212-982-5579
donahuesosinskiart@earthlink.net
http://www.artnet.com/donahue-sosinski .html.

Gallery Hours: Tuesday-Saturday 10-6
Slides available
Contact: Ronald Sosinski, Director

"Alfredo Martinez by David Greenberg" October, 1999

"The history of U.S. arms production is as sordid and soiled as certain blue Gap dresses. The history of U.S. sculpture is equally parasitic.
Alfredo Martinez, in a stroke of genius or madness (I suspect a little of both), has joined together these two disciplines.
He has created a sub-genre all his own."

Art in America October 1999 IMPORT/EXPORT Generation Z: Slacker Than Thou P.S.1, domestic debris and photographic self-portraits dominate an international exhibition of over 20 artists, almost all under the age of 35.
by Nancy Princenthal:

"What stood out in this welter of re-created workroom dishabille and compulsive self-reflection? The fully dressed, the tight-lipped and, above all, the hard working.

Alfredo Martinez, a 32-year-old New Yorker described as having been a private detective, arms dealer's assistant, weapons consultant for films and, at present, part-time gunsmith, weighed in with a pair of heavy-metal gladiators, in the Mad Max tradition, that gave (misleading) showbiz drama to the exhibition's entryway."

Alfredo Martinez

Guns and Drawings

Curated by: KENNY SCHACHTER

October 21 - November 20, 1999

DONAHUE / SOSINSKI ART

560 Broadway #304
New York, New York 10012
212-226-1111 (Fax) 212-982-5579
donahuesosinski@earthlink.net

Reception: Saturday, October 23, 7 - 10 pm

Arms and the man

The lumbering fatigue-wearing arms manufacturer **Alfredo Martinez**, is currently showing his new work at **Donahue/Sosinski** gallery. Martinez has a vision of the artist as gunsmith, making simulated rocket launchers out of PVC pipes and AK47s out of scrap metal and cookie tins. With weapon art from the elegant **Tom Sachs** and the nuclear **Gregory Green**, is the art world preparing for an insurgency?

For his show, Martinez transformed the gallery into a temporary studio space, filling it with a long wooden table and a myriad of tools, gear, scraps and assorted materials. On the wall were large raw primitivist drawings in a loose accurate hand in marker and ink, collaged with pages from illustrated gun magazines.

Alfredo Martinez
courtesy Donahue/Sosinski Gallery

Martinez likes to tell the story of **Joseph Beuys** telling the story of the famed

gangster **John Dillinger**, who escaped from prison after carving a small handgun from a bar of prison soap and blackening it with shoe polish. Here, Martinez carved a gun much like Dillinger did -- as if to put himself in a bad-boy lineage with an art historical context. It's as daring a feat as this agent provocateur has done in this fully loaded show.

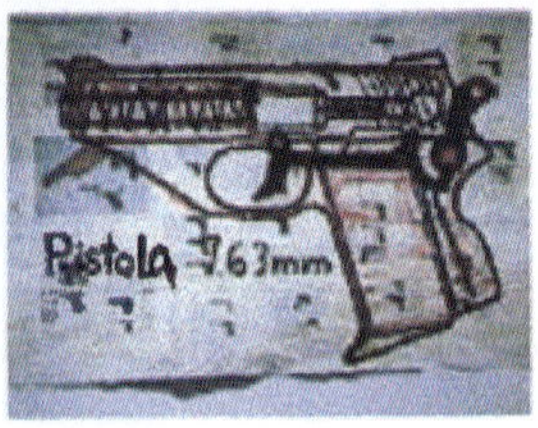

Alfredo Martinez
courtesy Donahue/Sosinski Gallery

MAX HENRY lives in New York City.

EMAIL LOGIN ▸ back to top

THE PROPOSITION
ELLEN DONAHUE AND RONALD SOSINSKI

Art in America

Alfredo Martinez at the Proposition

It's not uncommon for artists to inhabit galleries for the duration of their exhibitions nowadays, more often than not as a gesture that they mean business. Alfredo Martinez, on the other hand, consented to being locked in a gallery in 1999 because his dealer at the time had come to the realization that the artist, rather accustomed to living by the seat of his pants, could not otherwise be trusted to finish making art in a timely manner. So, in a sense, it's fortuitous that Martinez—now 36—has been dwelling in prison since 2002, where he has managed to create an impressive body of work for his latest exhibition, "The United States vs. Alfredo Martinez." It included 34 drawings (the largest is 8 by 5 feet), a few sculptures, a film of the artist at work, some court documents and 13 cassette tapes of Martinez speaking with an undercover FBI agent who purchased Basquiat paintings that Martinez forged, sold and are the reason for his incarceration.

Martinez ran away from his Brooklyn family at 18 and found some stability among the habitués of Keith Haring's studio. He became friends with Jean-Michel Basquiat and had stints working as a studio assistant for both Donald Baechler and fellow firearm fanatic Tom Sachs. One of several downtown Manhattan artists obsessed with and able to construct functioning guns from raw materials, Martinez instantly got busy behind bars rendering various models of automatic weapons on sheets of paper that he made from saved paper scraps and homemade glue. Mediums ranged from coffee and Kool-Aid to pencil and ink. In fact, the drawings were so disturbingly accurate that prison officials identified Martinez as a terrorist and confiscated his art supplies.

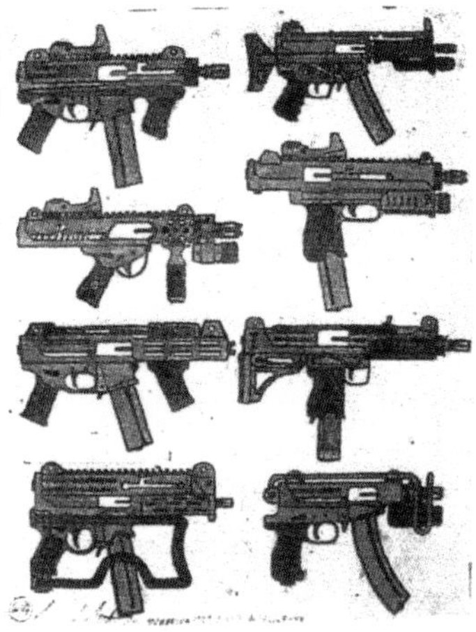

Alfredo Martinez: *Untitled #20*, 2003, coffee and mixed mediums on handmade paper, 28 by 22 inches; at the Proposition.

Martinez responded by hiring a lawyer and staging a hunger strike that lasted 55 days and ended with his being fed by force. His art-making materials were returned to him, and he resumed creating intriguing creepy drawings. Some include text. "I will not let th bastards win," reads one self-portrait. Another piece hosts the cryptic declaratio "I've belonged to a militant cats' group for ages I'm tru to my specious! [*sic*]."

There were also several portraits of Martinez's fello inmates, mostly thuggish-looking black men. He dre Gene Simmons, the leade of the heavy-metal band Kiss, as well as televangelist Billy Graham—here imagined with flesh falling off his face and an eyeball popping out of his skull. The most compelling work in the show are labor-inten sive montages of symbols that seem to represent Martinez's bizarre, badass cosmology. Among his ciphers are Christ, pentagrams, anarc symbols, and logos for the punk bands GBH and Dead Kennedys. A diagram in one piece appears to illustrate something about the end of th world. It reads: "death of the su does not affect us immediately because we are not in its futur outcome."

Cleverly installed in a small rear gallery, so as to maximize potential to scare people, was a larger-than-human sculpture (2001) of a pig/man toting a machine gun. It tended to make people jump when they entered the room.

Indeed, Martinez's main taler as an artist is to spook people, get them wondering whether or not he's truly out of his mind, unable to distinguish between reality and fantasy. He lives his work, raises the stakes, and makes art seem as unsafe and exciting as we might actually want it to be. —*Sarah Vald*

ARSENAL FOR DEMOCRACY
WAR CORPORATISM

JANUARY 27 - FEBRUARY 24TH, 2006

ALFREDO MARTINEZ

EXHIBIT OPENING
8-10PM
FRIDAY, JANUARY 27TH

RSVP: RSVP@1134NYC.COM

THE CANAL CHAPTER
343 CANAL ST.
4TH FLOOR
BETWEEN GREEN ST. & WOOSTER ST.
NEW YORK

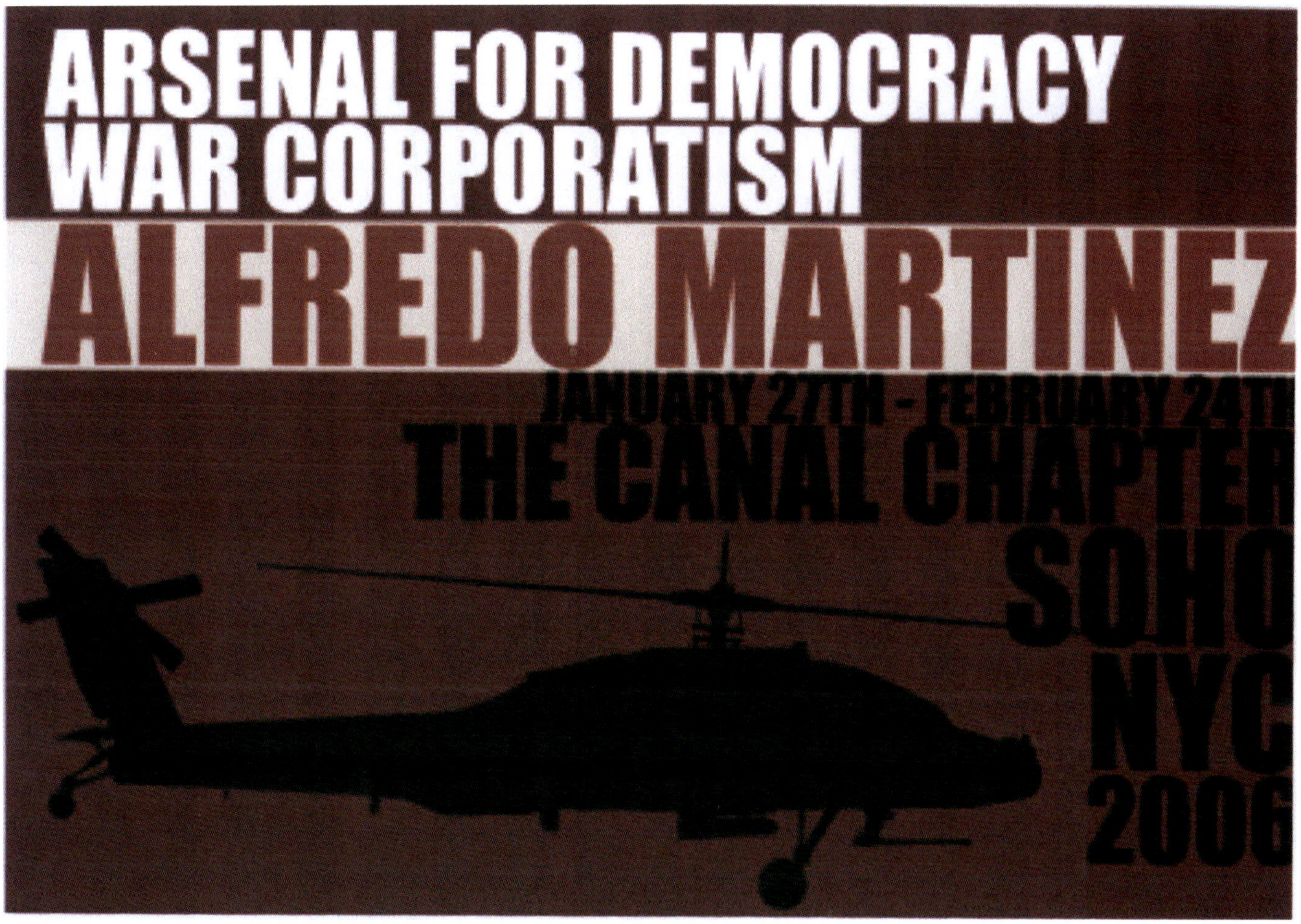
ARSENAL FOR DEMOCRACY
WAR CORPORATISM
ALFREDO MARTINEZ
JANUARY 27TH - FEBRUARY 24TH
THE CANAL CHAPTER
SOHO
NYC
2006

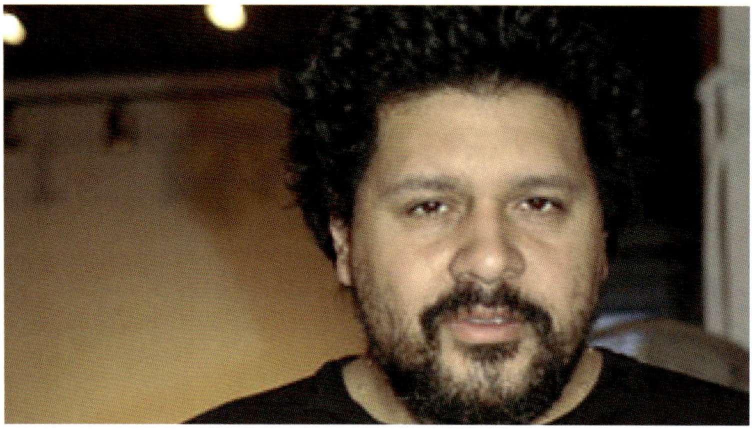

passport, but he threw out the drawings. If I'd seen him I would have murdered him. Then I went to Morris King and I got hassled immediately at the door by security. I was like 'I'm here to get my passport.' Anyway, I got past them and freaked out on the people at Morris King. "You paid him but you didn't get my drawings?'"

So those drawings are gone for good. It was time to get around to what really happened in China. Alfredo was living at his secret lair (a brand new but already falling apart pseudo-Bauhaus gallery building with incongruous round windows commonly known as "That porthole place") but was mostly hanging out at an internet café with air conditioning down by Wangfujing. Before we went ahead I asked if he really wanted to talk about his experience in jail there or if it would be too unpleasant. He said he would, and compared it to the 21 months he spent in federal prison in the United States on a wire fraud charge connected to forging Basquiat paintings.

"As far as jail, it freaked me out because it was the first time I felt like I was really not in control," he said. I asked him if he felt in control while jailed in the US. "I was completely working the system. I had an angle. I was a kind of hero there because I was getting one over on them. The only residue of that experience is that now when I smell Insure, it smells like baby formula, and now when I smell baby formula–because that's what they force fed me with–the smell makes me want to retch. That's the only real psychological tick I have from all that."

"OK, but what happened in Beijing?"

"A friend of mine there wanted to make a sculpture, like a portable nuclear launcher, it's about the size of a bazooka. It's called the Davy Crocket. When I got arrested at the internet cafe I was downloading theses Davy Crocket plans. There were three guys–they looked like they were in Iraq. Black army uniforms, and one guy had a sub-machine gun. Military police. Luckily when I saw them I was able to reboot the computer so all the files got erased, but that made them angry. The main guy made me nervous with his smile. It was like when I suck in my stomach when I see a pretty girl–it's so not genuine. They took me outside, put a black hood over my head and put me in a black van. When we got to the place–the prison–it got so heavy I didn't want to tell them shit. I was in Brooklyn mode: don't be a rat. I was alone in the cell and the temperature was really cold and the bed was a concrete block with a straw mat. The cold made me always uncomfortable, and I got a really bad cough and then really sick."

"They kept asking me to confess but I wouldn't. I said I'm an artist. Anyway, the sicker I got, the more worried they got. I couldn't bathe and I was sure they were putting drugs in my food, so I stopped eating. It might have been ten days, it might have been longer. Then one day they had me look at a computer and they asked, 'Is that you?' They had Googled my name. They told me 'You have many friends looking for you.' I think they were like, 'He's American, we fucked up.' So they took me to another prison, a medical one. I was really sick. When we got there a big fight erupted between the two commanders." Basically, the commander of the new prison didn't want him, which in retrospect is totally understandable.

"I know they were thinking, 'Look at this nigger; we don't want him dying on our watch!' The guys who dropped me off didn't want to sign anything. A doctor looked at me and took my blood pressure every day. I started feeling better and they were treating me better. They tried to give me special food but I wanted to eat the same food everybody else was getting, so I made them give the other prisoners that food too. The Chinese authorities told me they would deport me and waive the fine for overstaying my visa, but I would have to tell the embassy they treated me well. 'We can have you on a plane tomorrow,' they said. Eventually a girl from the embassy came. She was cute, wearing a little Prada outfit. I didn't complain and I feel kind of shitty about that."

A day later he was driven straight to the airport where Byron gave him the drawings, a pair of size 14 sneakers, and some clothes. He was put on a flight through Dubai to New York. "I got back to New York and I was like, 'I need a teaching job, no more adventuring!'"

So a near death experience (or so it certainly must have seemed at the time), or at the very least a harrowing and no fun at all experience. That had been made crystal clear to me the first time I'd seen Alfredo upon his return, a week and a half prior to the conversation recorded here. That day his much more vivid and jangled version of events gave an unmistakable air of veracity to his report, as did his overall countenance–that of a genuinely rattled (and completely justifiable) basket case telling his story in disjointed bits and pieces. While he was relating what had happened in a much less measured manner than how he did ten days later I bought him two burritos at a taco truck parked at North 7th and Bedford. How weird is that? North 7th and Bedford after three years in China and three weeks in Chinese prison. When he got to the part about the hood being put over his head a nondescript concerned citizen sitting on a bench munching his tacos next to us piped in with, "Excuse me, why did they put a hood over your head?" As he recalled later, "I bit that poor guy's head off. He was some white marketing executive. Why didn't he mind his own business? He thought we were all friends or something. The rule of New York is if you hear something, you don't interject. I was about to punch him." I can definitively say he appeared to be very ready to do that. It was a tense, uncomfortable moment. And as I guided and sort of ushered Alfredo away the guy looked like he was about to have a heart attack. Which he would have deserved. But now things seem mellower. Those drawings might be lost for good and Alfredo can never ever go back to China, but he's making new work, he's busy, he's hustling, and maybe now things will calm down. Or maybe they'll start all over again.

JOCKO WEYLAND

Tuesday, March 8, 2011 at 2:56 pm by JOCKO WEYLAND VICE US
Tags: art, China, raw china

« PREVIOUS POST VICELAND TODAY NEXT POST »

Comments

Anonymous, on Mar 9, 2011 *wrote:*
this guy sounds like the smartest, coolest guy in the world. he totally "gamed the system" in the united states and was in control the whole time and then he forced the chinese prison system to treat their inmates better, all while rejecting the advances of chinese women who he was too good for. he also totally took the word of a paranoid weirdo that they were going to shoot him in guatemala which PROBABLY SAVED HIS AWESOME LIFE.

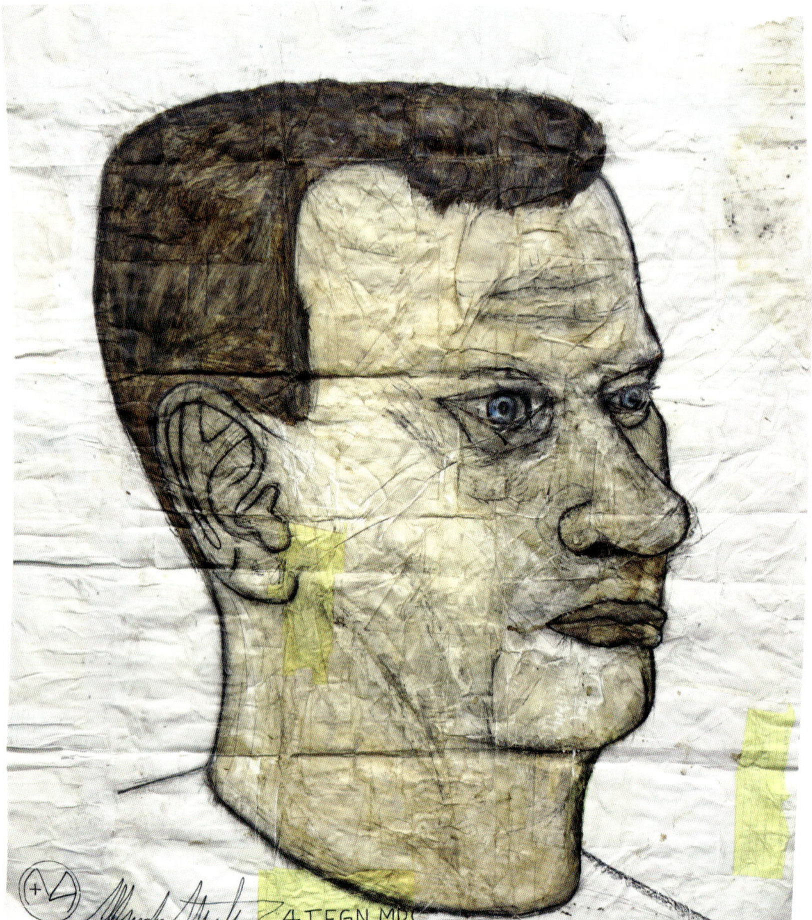

Prisoner Portrait #1

2002

Mixed Media on Hand Collaged Paper

42 x 38 in.

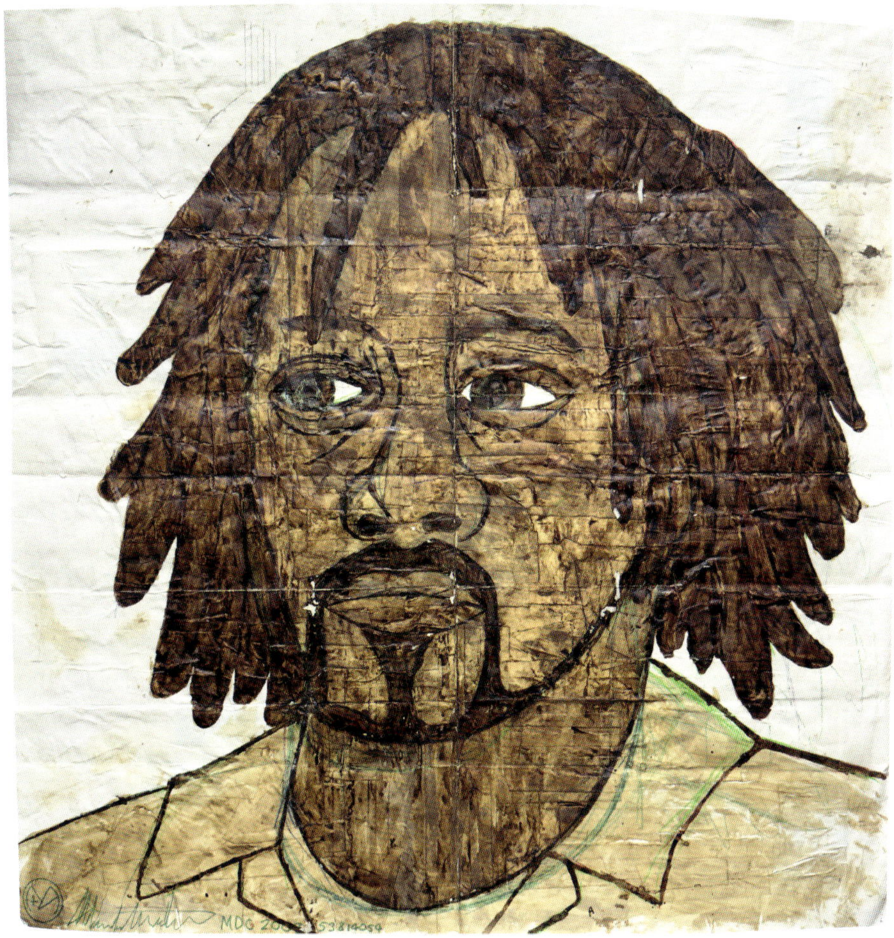

Prisoner Portrait #2

2002

Mixed Media on Hand Collaged Paper

42 x 40 in.

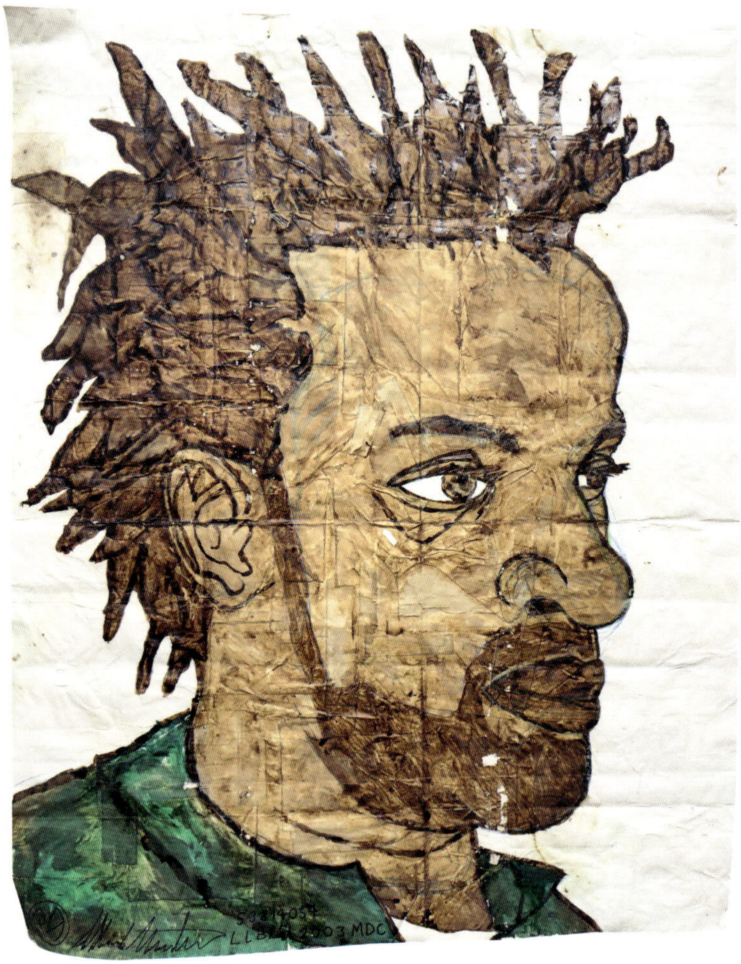

Prisoner Portrait #3

2004

Mixed Media on Hand Collaged Paper

44 x 39 in.

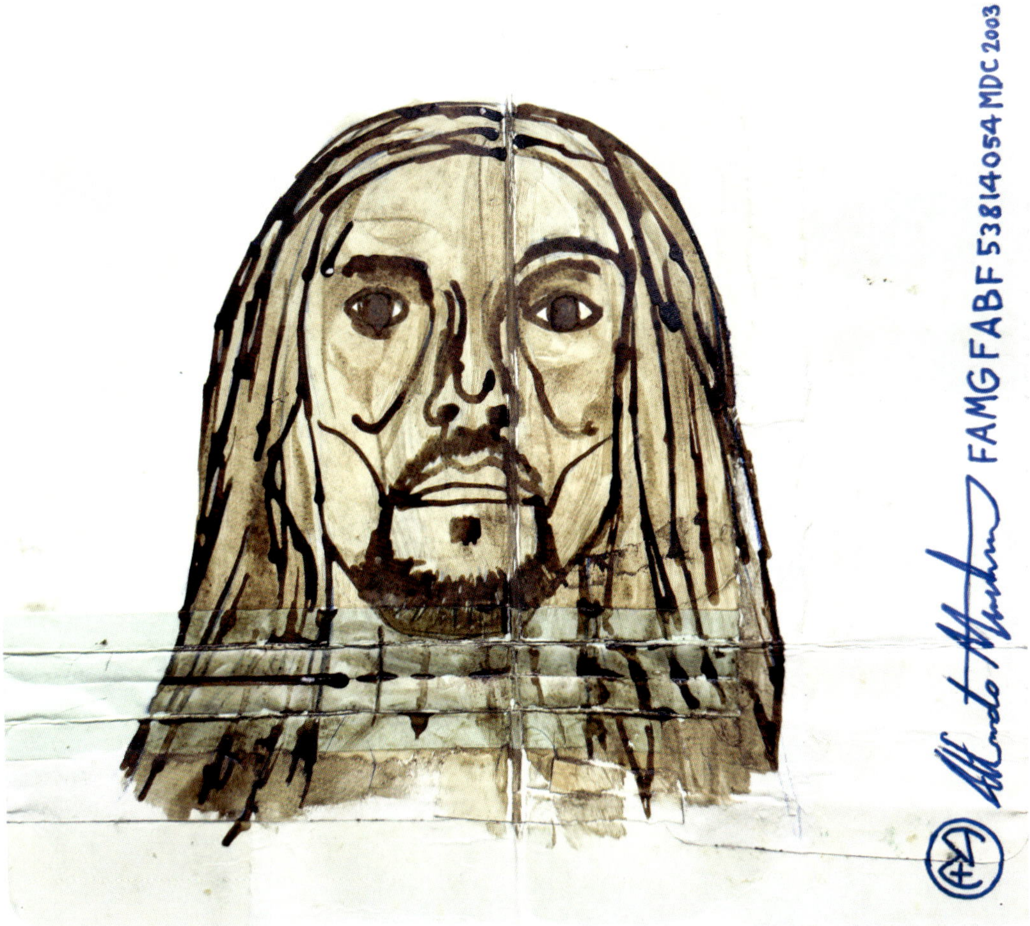

Prisoner Portrait #4

2003

Mixed Media on Hand Collaged Paper

14 x 16 in.

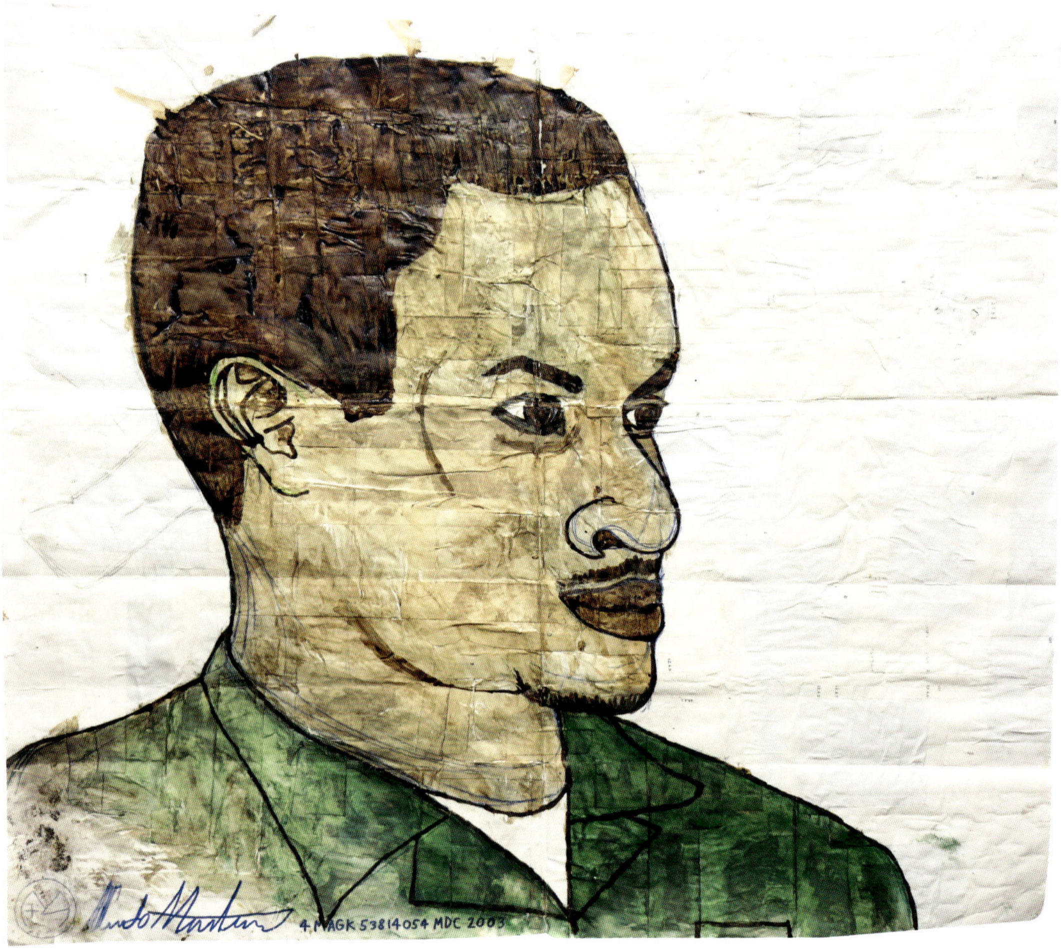

Prisoner Portrait #5

2003

Mixed Media on Hand Collaged Paper

34 x 40 in.

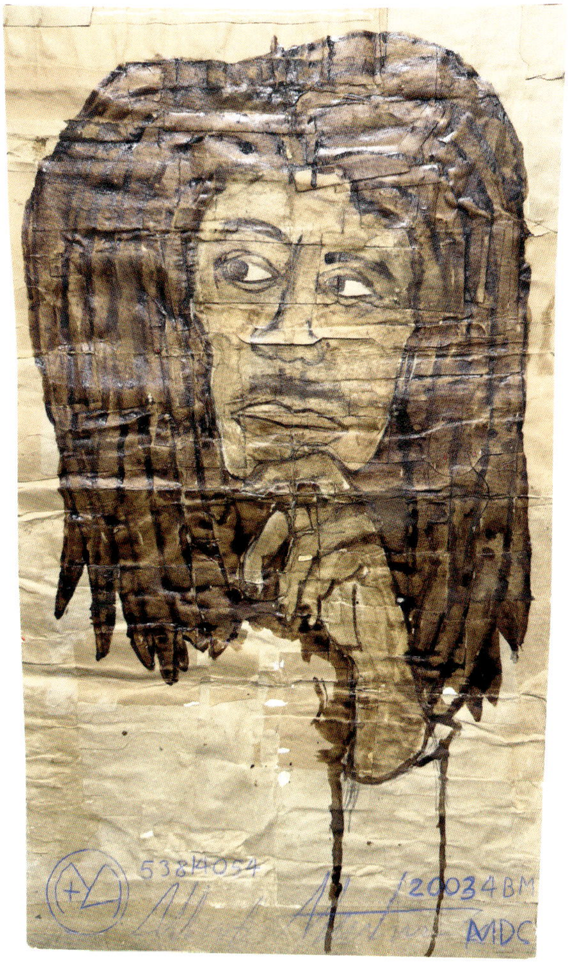

Bob Marley Portrait

2003

Mixed Media on Hand Collaged Paper

24 x 14.5 in.

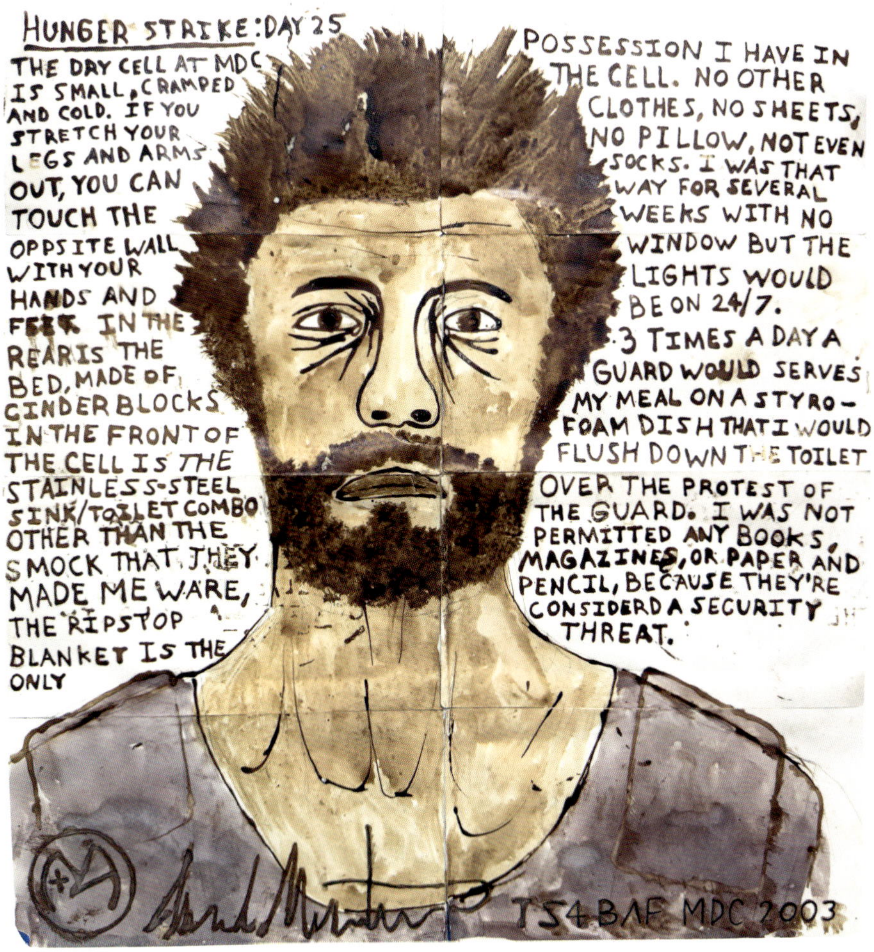

Prison Self Portrait

2003

Mixed Media on Hand Collaged Paper

19 x 18 in.

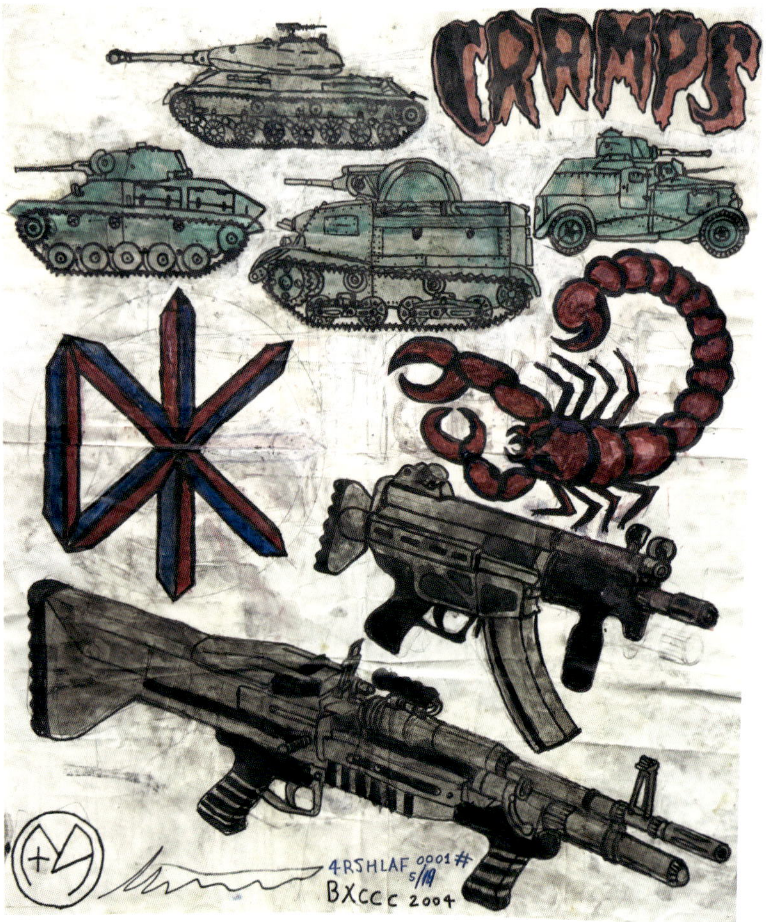

Cramps

2004

Mixed Media on Hand Collaged Paper

29 x 24 in.

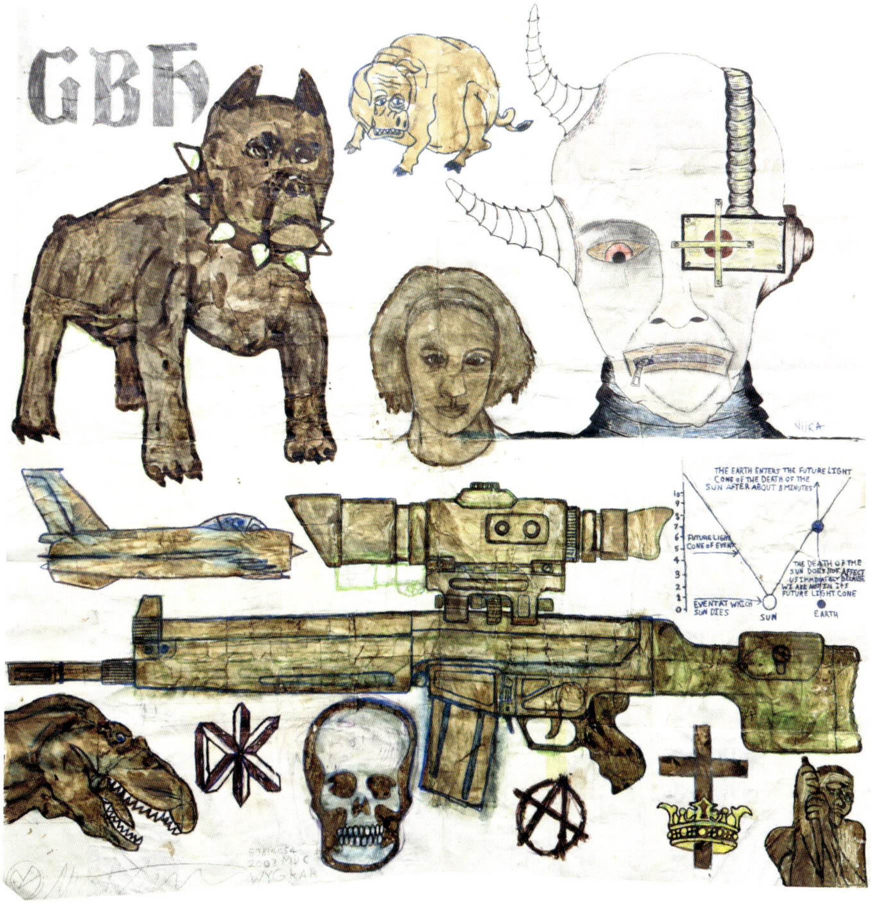

GBH

2003

Mixed Media on Hand Collaged Paper

40 x 40 in.

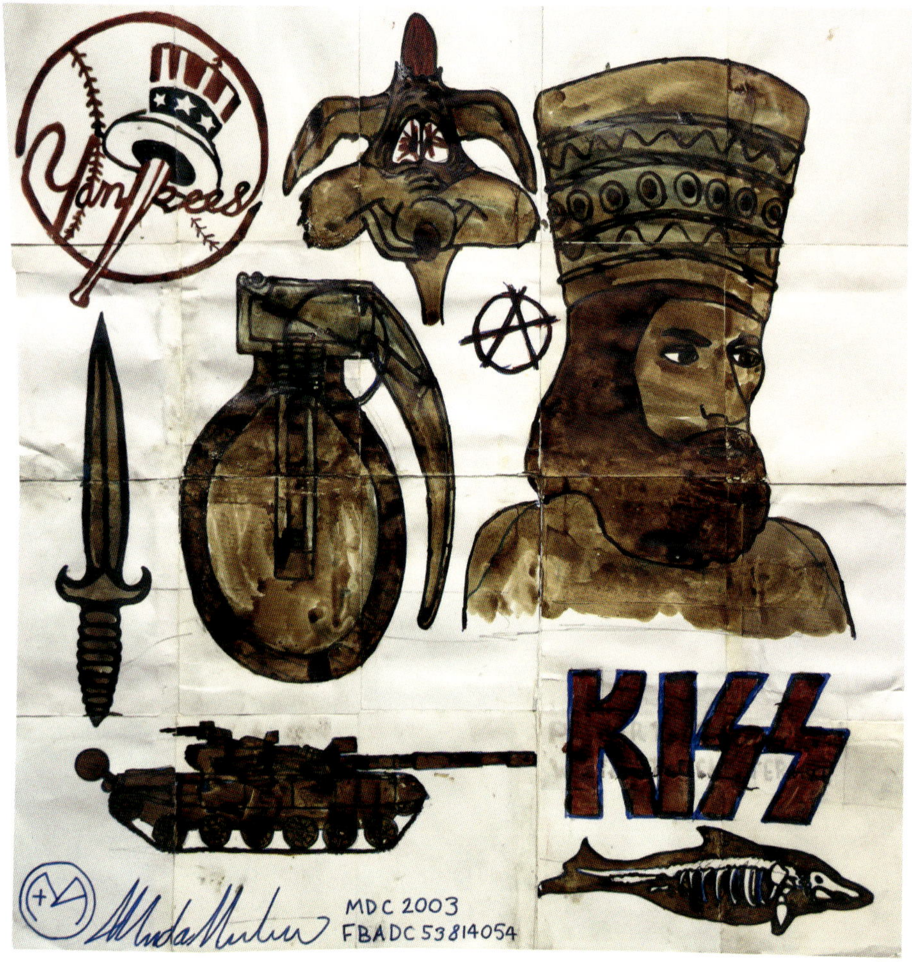

Kiss

2004

Mixed Media on Hand Collaged Paper

24 x 23 in.

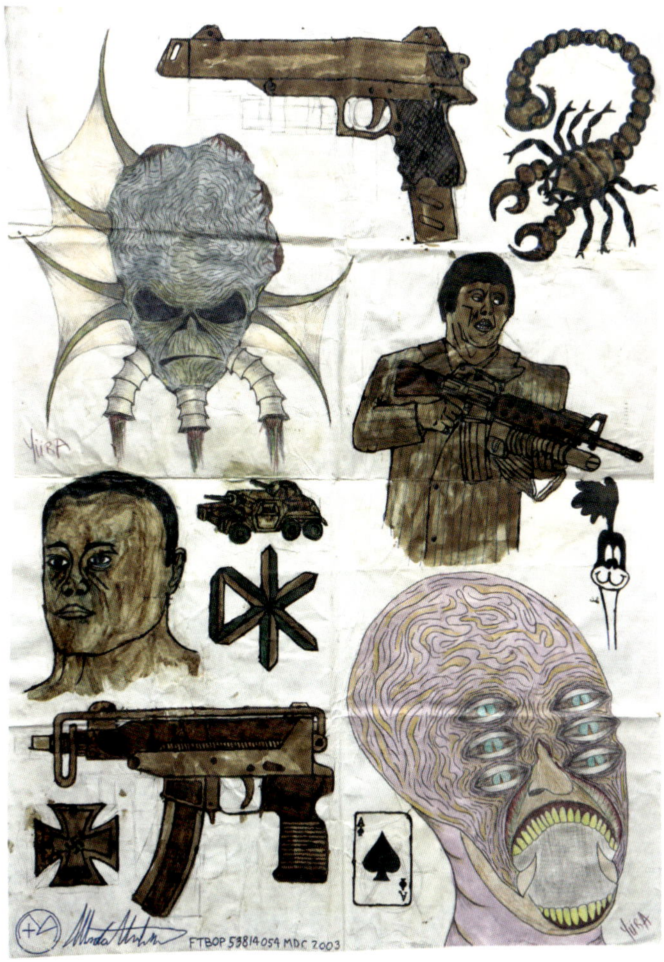

Scream

2003

Mixed Media on Hand Collaged Paper

40 x 40 in.

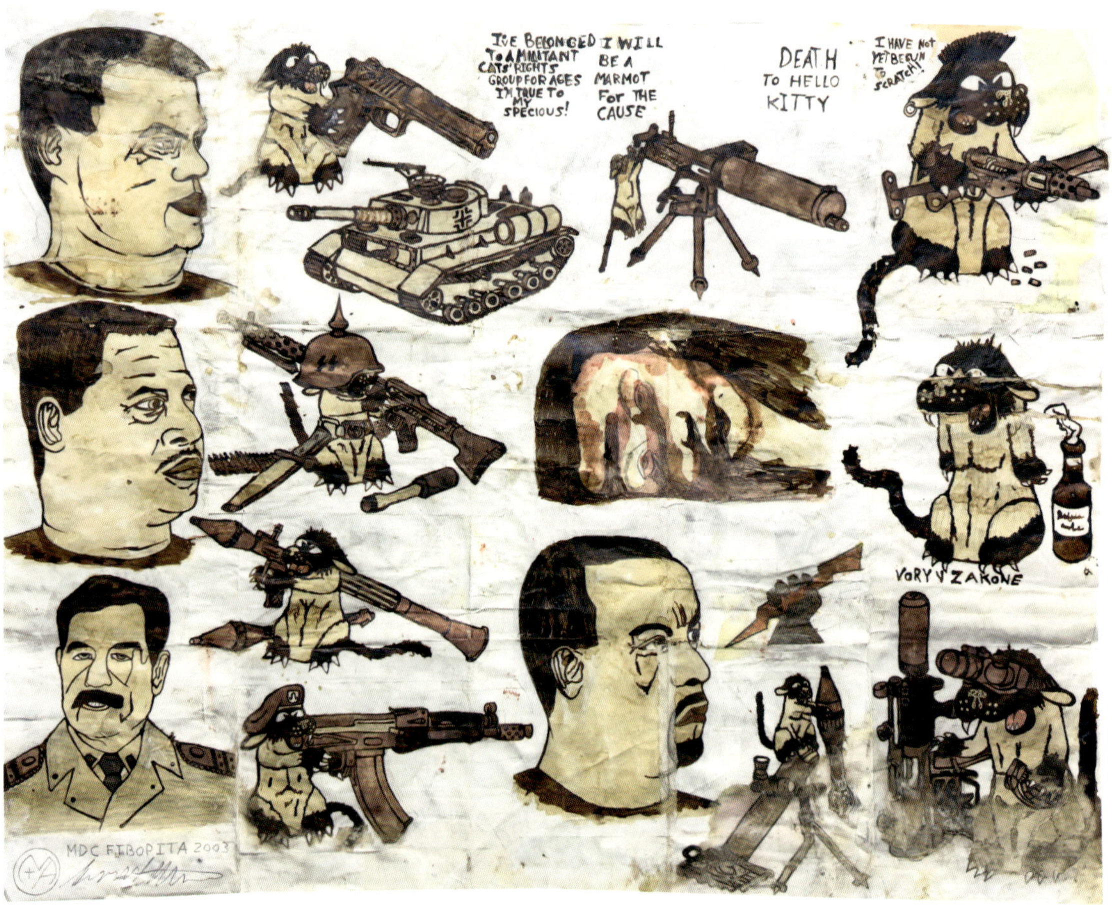

Sadam Drawing

2003

Mixed Media on Hand Collaged Paper

31.5 x 40.5 in.

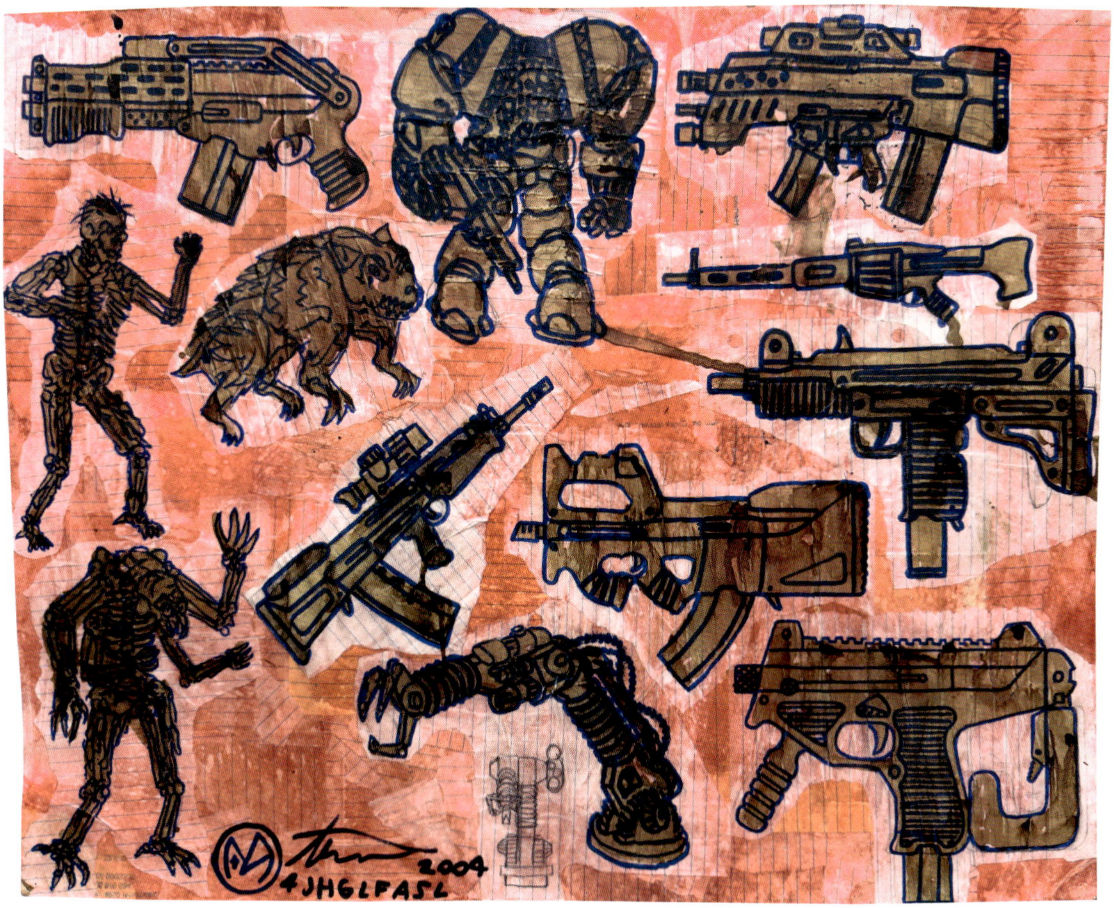

Red Drawing

2004

Mixed Media on Hand Collaged Paper

22 x 27 in.

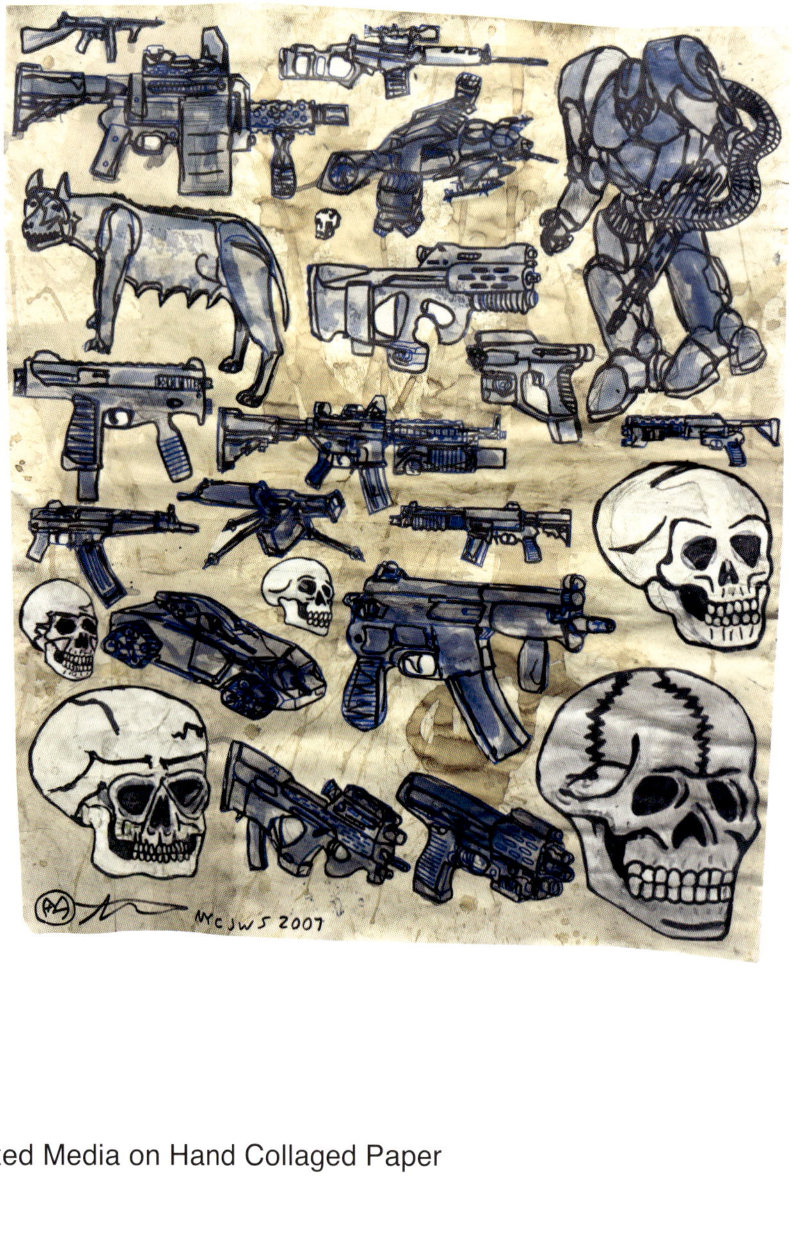

Drawing #1

2007

Multi-Image/Mixed Media on Hand Collaged Paper

38 x 29 in.

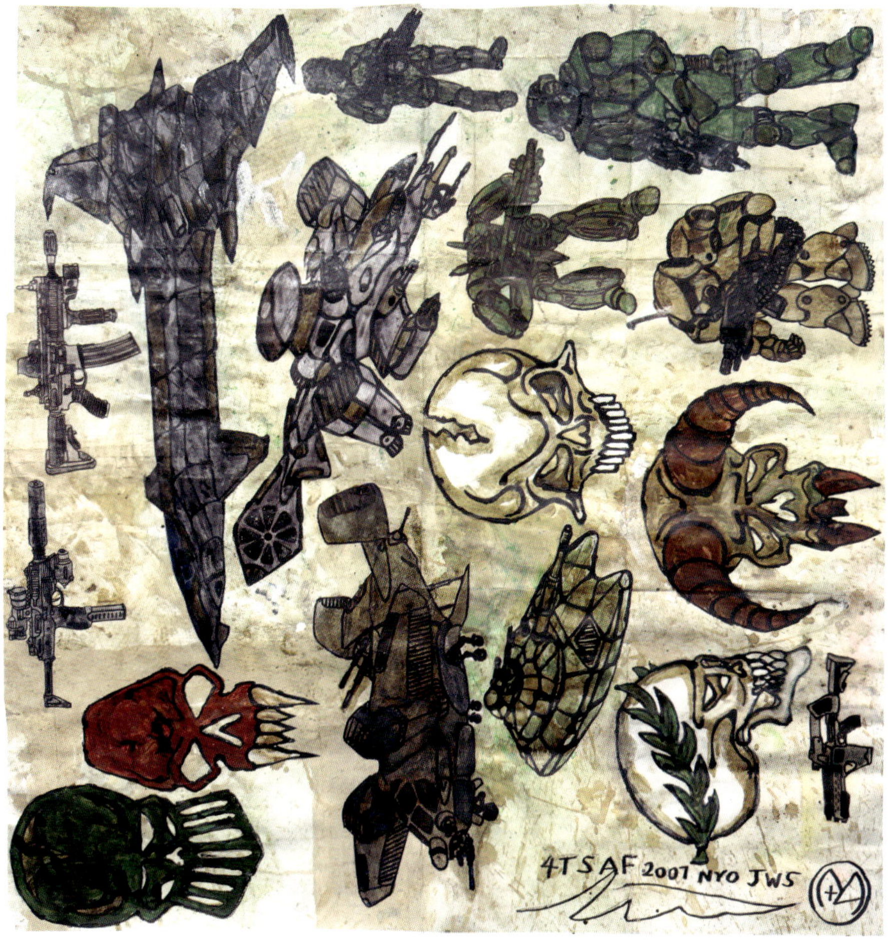

Drawing #2
2007
Multi-Image/Mixed Media on Hand Collaged Paper
38 x 38 in.

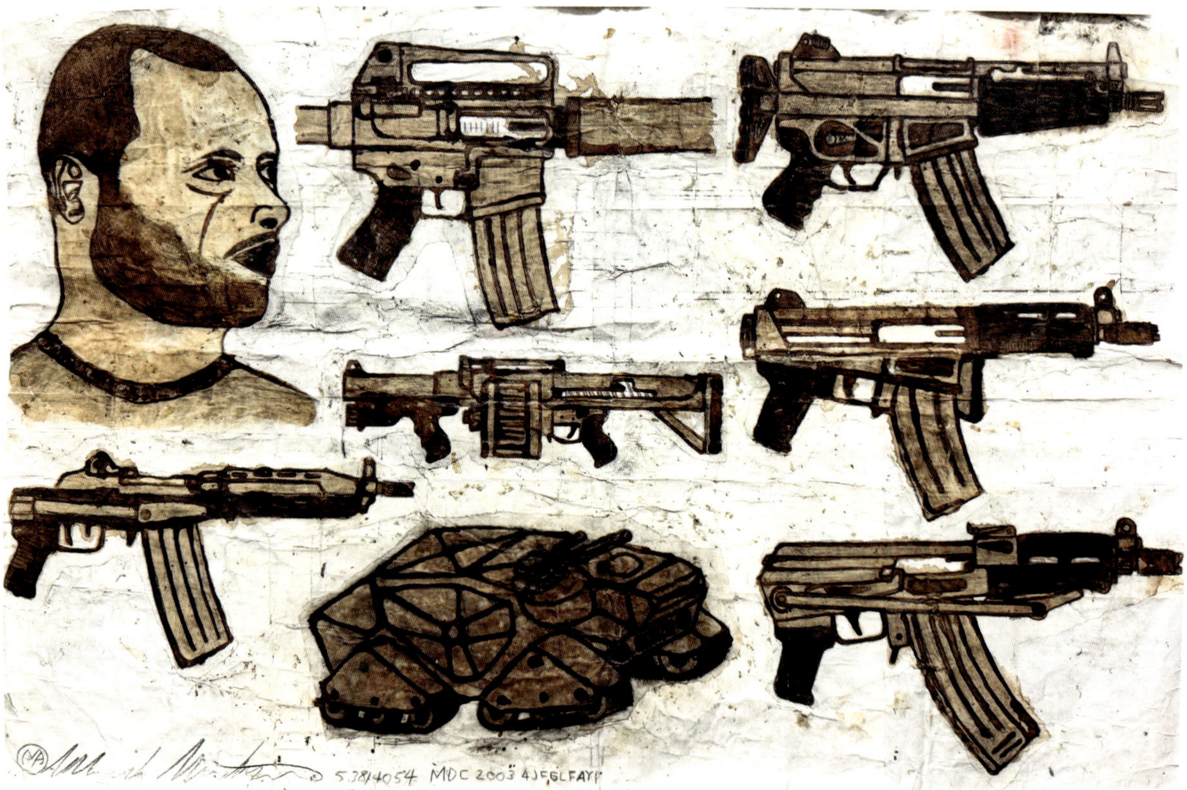

Drawing #3

2003

Multi-Image/Mixed Media on Hand Collaged Paper

29 x 37 in.

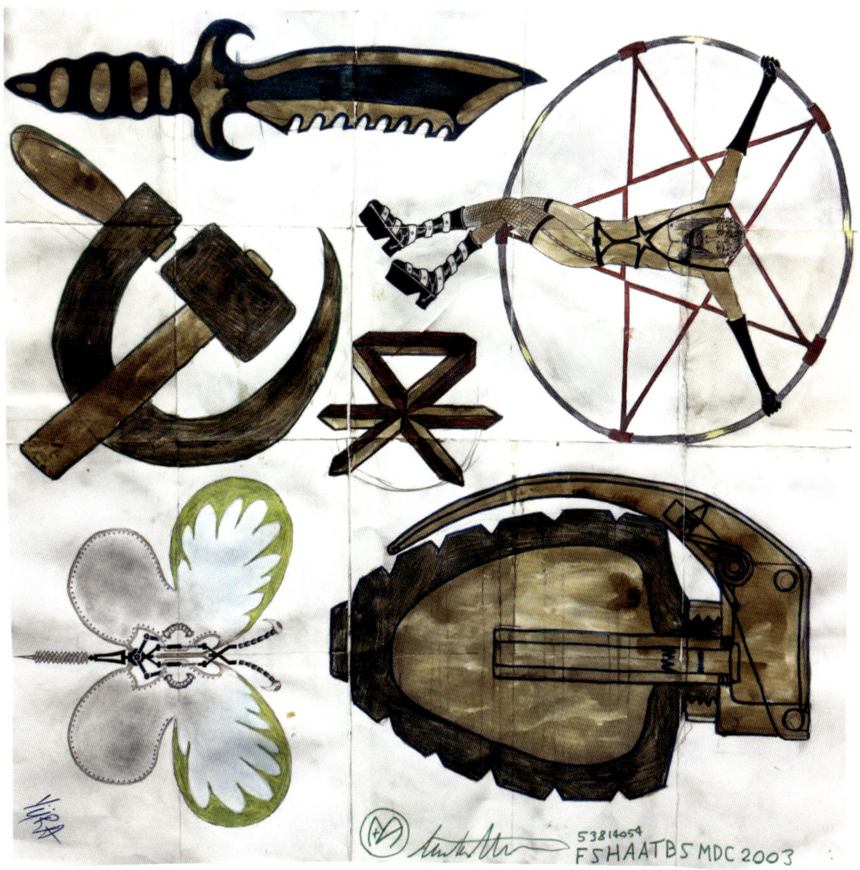

Drawing #4

2003

Multi-Image/Mixed Media on Hand Collaged Paper

24 x 24 in.

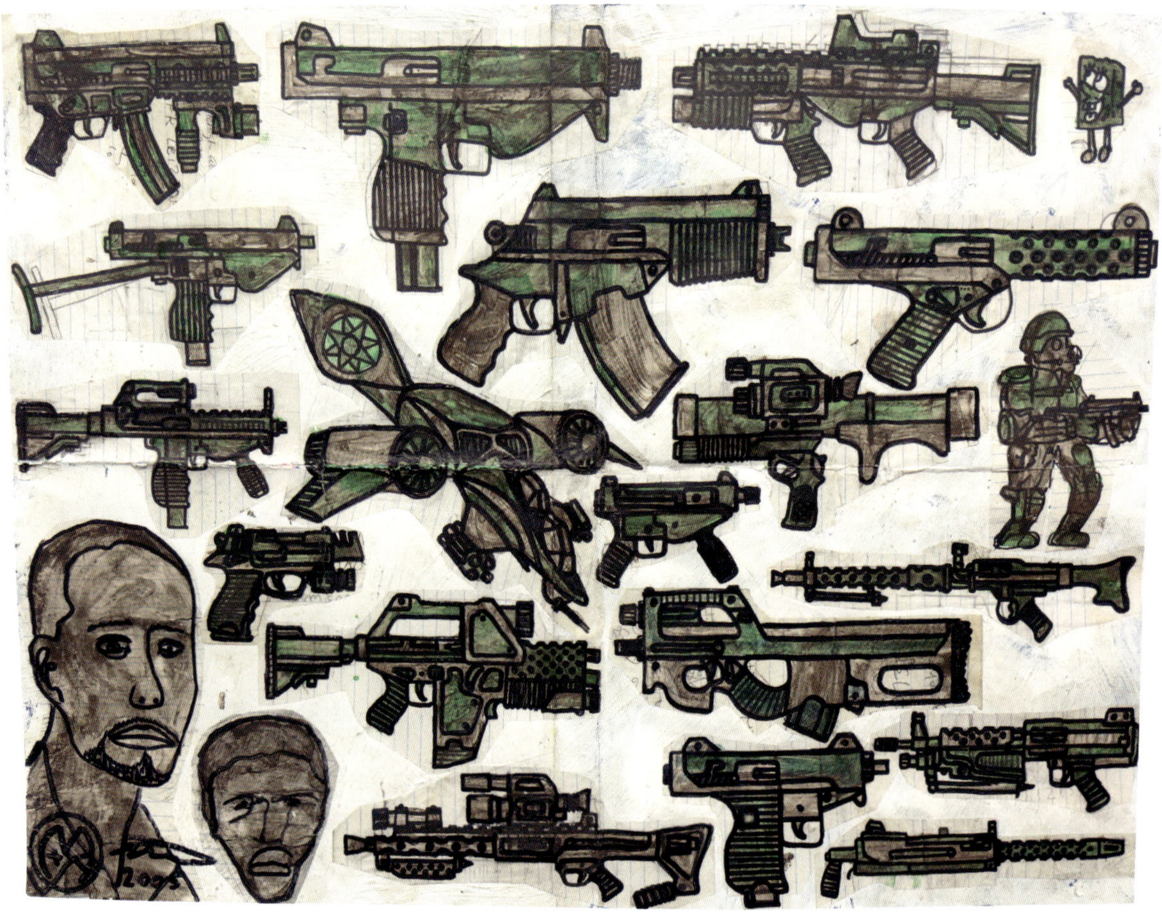

Drawing #5

2003

Multi-Image/Mixed Media on Hand Collaged Paper

22 x 29 in.

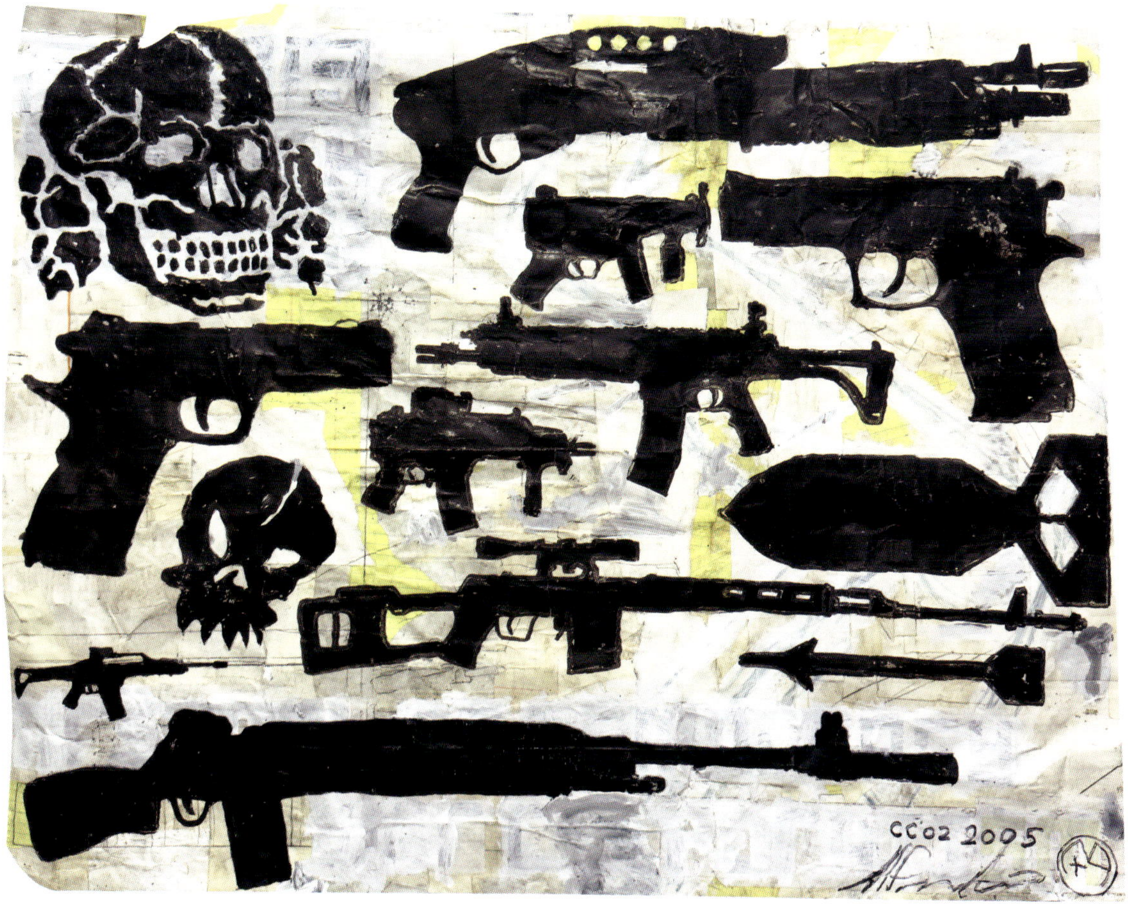

Black
2005
Multi-Image/Mixed Media on Hand Collaged Paper
29 x 37 in.

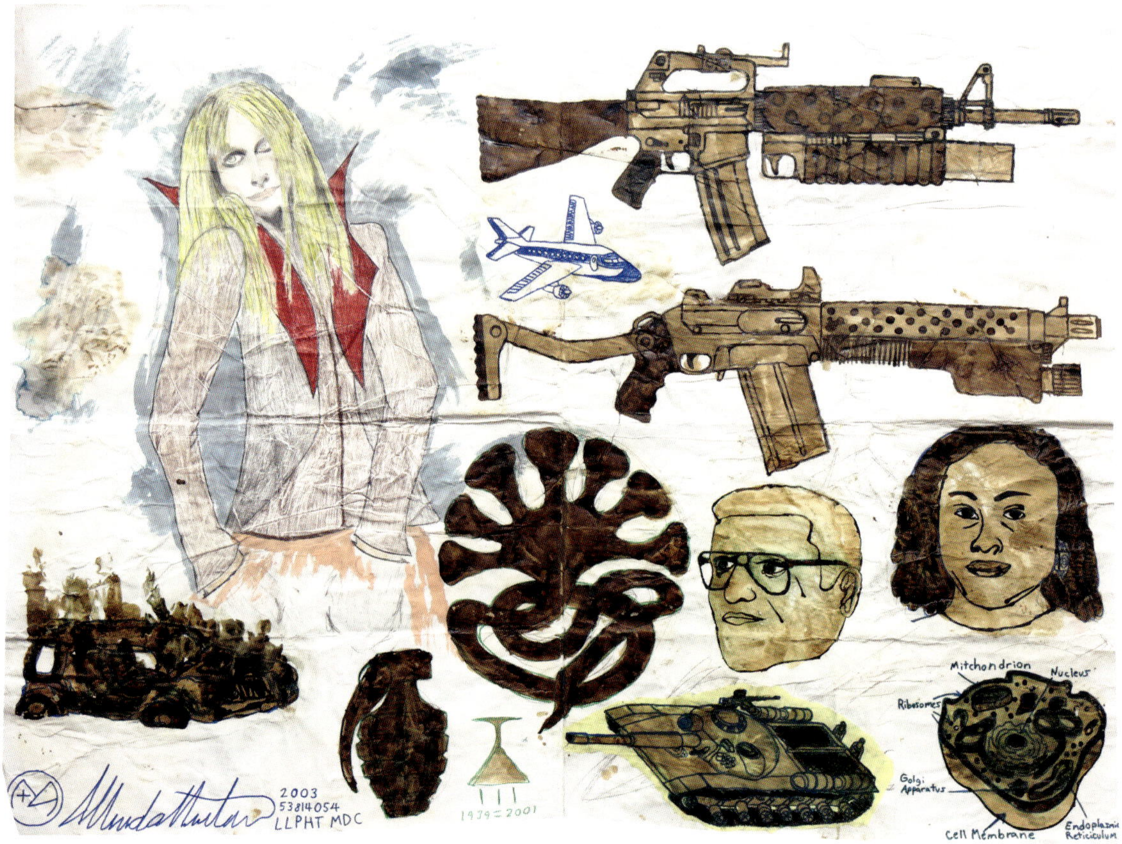

Drawing #6

2005

Multi-Image/Mixed Media on Hand Collaged Paper

29 x 41 in.

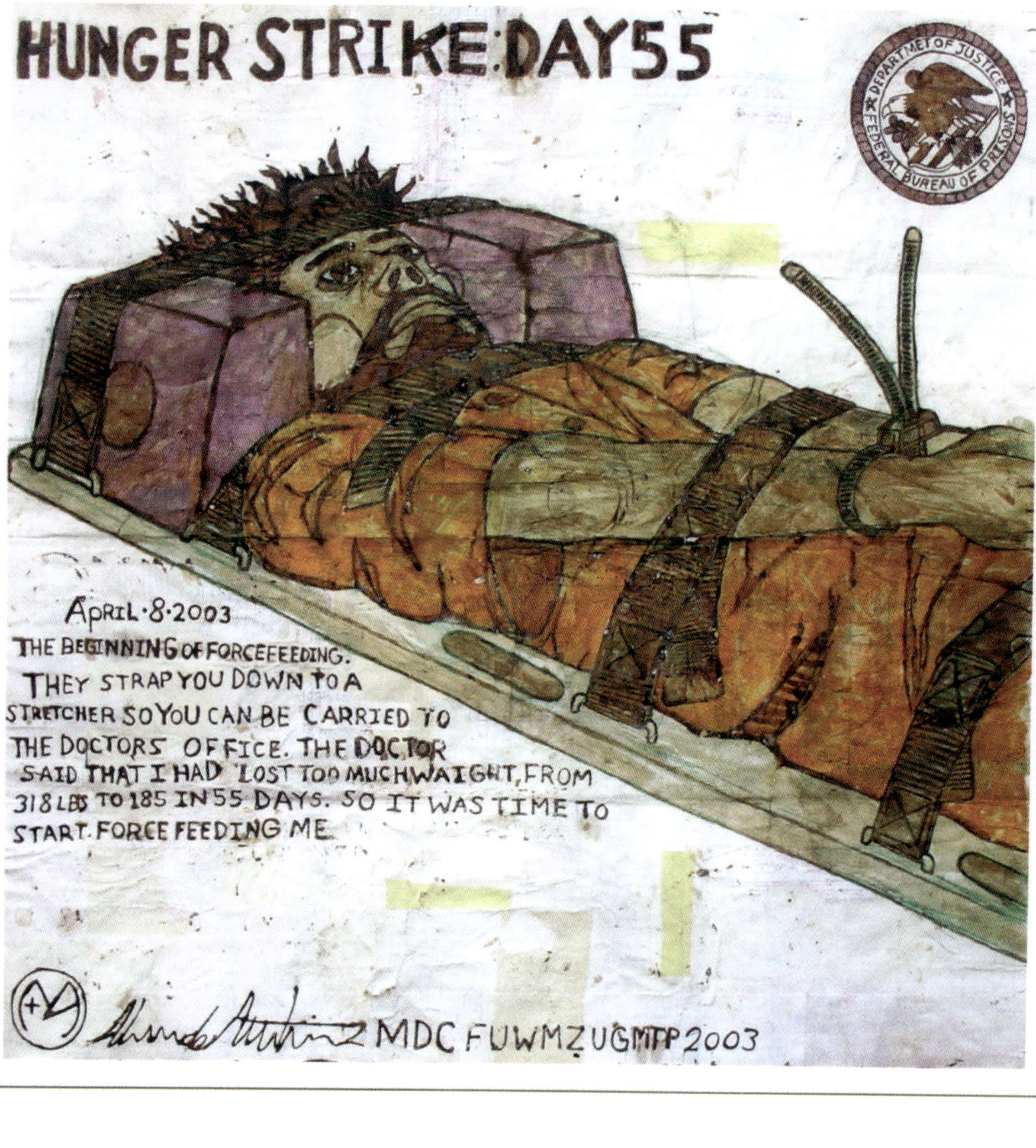
HUNGER STRIKE:DAY55
DEPARTMET OF JUSTICE
FEDERAL BUREAU OF PRISONS
APRIL·8·2003
THE BEGINNING OF FORCEFEEDING.
THEY STRAP YOU DOWN TO A
STRETCHER SO YOU CAN BE CARRIED TO
THE DOCTORS OFFICE. THE DOCTOR
SAID THAT I HAD LOST TOO MUCH WAIGHT, FROM
318 LBS TO 185 IN 55 DAYS. SO IT WAS TIME TO
START FORCE FEEDING ME
MDC FUWMZUGMTP 2003

Alfredo Martinez
Inmate #53814054
MDC UNIT H53
P.O. BoX 329003
Brooklyn, NY, 11232

BROOKLYN NY 11256
PM
05 MAR
2004

USA 37

Ron Sosinski
559 WEST 22nd St
2nd Floor
NYC NY 10011

10011/1138

THE PROPOSITION

FOR IMMEDIATE RELEASE

ALFREDO MARTINEZ

VINTAGE PRISON DRAWINGS / NEW WORK FROM BEIJING

The Proposition is pleased to present our inaugural virtual exhibitions, *Vintage Prison Drawings* and *New Work From Beijing*, both highlighting the work of artist Alfredo Martinez. *Vintage Prison Drawings* will focus on Martinez' output from 2002-2004 with pieces encapsulating his stint in federal prison after being convicted on charges stemming from his forgings of Basquiat drawings and their corresponding certificates of authenticity, while *New Work From Beijing* features some of his most recent drawings produced while living in Beijing, China. Both exhibitions are scheduled in conjunction with Martinez' participation and appearance in the Sundance Grand Jury Prize-winning documentary feature-film, *We Live in Public*, directed by Ondi Timoner and screening on April 5th, 2009, as the closing film of MoMA's 2009 *New Directors / New Films* series.

In December 1999, as a participant in the millennial project, *Quiet* - an epic event organized and financed by dot-com millionaire Josh Harris involving dozens of artists occupying an underground bunker on lower Broadway, voluntarily subjecting themselves to interrogations and constant surveillance for up to thirty days before FEMA intervened and put an end to the so-called "Millennial-Cult" - Martinez designed a full-size indoor firing range, complete with sound-proofing and furnished with high-powered automatic weapons and a staff of ex-Navy Seals. Now, almost ten years later, *Quiet* has been documented and condensed into the arc of the story-line encompassing *We Live in Public*, Ondi Timoner's film chronicling the trajectory of Josh Harris' life and obsession with media consumption in the age of the internet.

Alfredo Martinez has often utilized guns and weaponry in his imagery and they remain a primary focal point of many of his drawings/collaged-paper compositions and prints. He has constructed both small and large-scale sculptures out of a wide variety of industrial materials to create guns, including some that are fully functional as a result of his weapons background and experience acquired from years of working with Rick Washburn at Weapons Specialists Limited. This is also evidenced in some of his drawings, which appear as schematic diagrams of guns, offering x-ray views of their inner parts and components.

Martinez' drawings from prison range from self-portraits and portraits of fellow inmates to political figures, like Saddam Hussein, to guns and weapons, all of which were created by drawing with pencil on hand-collaged paper that he assembled from pages torn from books and various other sources and using prison-issued coffee & fruit punch as watercolor pigments – the only materials made available to him during his sentence. His most recent work from Beijing finds Martinez continuing with his fascination with weapons and includes yet another facet, featuring an increasingly technological bent with a focus on military machines and devices. In these he has incorporated actual cutouts of uniformed officers manning monitors and of robots and machines right alongside his drawings.

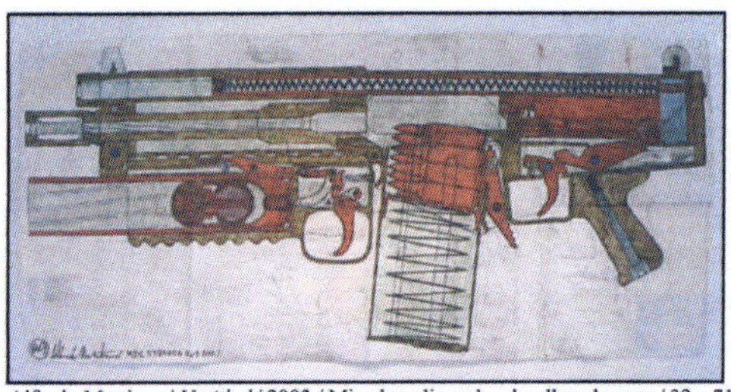

Alfredo Martinez / *Untitled* / 2003 / Mixed media on hand-collaged paper / 32 x 71"

Martinez currently resides in Beijing and has been living there since 2007. While in Beijing he has had work exhibited in the group show, *Surge*, at the Main Exhibition Space in the 798 Art District and he has curated a group show, *Dream Palace* at A-SPACE.

For additional information please contact Ronald Sosinski at 212.242.0035 or info@theproposition.com.

THE PROPOSITION
559 West 22nd Street
New York, New York 10011
T: 212-242-0035 -F: 212-242-0203
email: donahuesosinski@earthlink.net
www.theproposition.com

THE UNITED STATES OF AMERICA VS. ALFREDO MARTINEZ

Drawings from Prison

Curated by James Fuentes
Documentary Photos by Nancy Smith

October 24 - November 29, 2003
Reception: Friday, October 24, 6-8pm

scope Miami

NADA (New Art Dealers Alliance)
Miami, December 4-7

Printed By: www.4over4.com

1/9/04

Dear Ron

Would you give this friend of ours $100.00 I had to get stamps early so I can mail things out as soon as possable, They got 2 more Darwing and the guards throw out my art supplys when ever they can. I think the "NEW York Magazine" Thing got to them a little. They Have been fucking with the inmates in my unit a Lot now (Keeping the inmate Locked in there cell for 5 hrs more than normale and not Letting them cook, and now no one has been getting books for the Last 3 months and the guards have made it Clear that it is be because of me, so if they can not get me they with make it harsher for all the inmate in this unit hoping somthing bad will happen. But Do not worry, the Inmates are the only reson I can make any art at all in the prison, The inmates keep me suppled with all I need (The prison may not Lett me buy stamps so this my be the only way I can get any) It's a little endbaressing for people to help you so much with being able to do any-thing for them, but the inmates all tell me to keep going, thats all they want. I have about 18 Drawing started (I had help) hoping to have them Done Mon or Wen, I think its Better to have things in the mail as soon as I am done with them.

Love and be well

P.S. Sorry can't talk on Phone

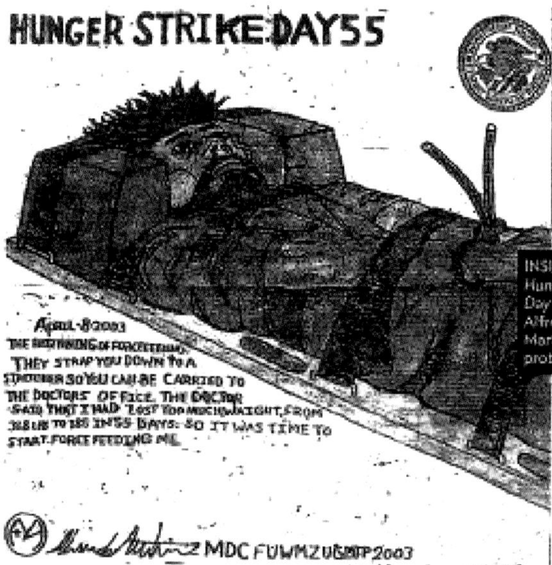

INSIDER ART: *Hunger Strike Day 55*, from Alfredo Martinez's first protest in prison.

JAILHOUSE NEWS

The Hunger Artist

A jailed Basquiat faker goes without food so that he can make (and sell) art. **By Anthony Haden-Guest**

"I'M GOING BACK ON hunger strike," Alfredo Martinez said during a call from Brooklyn's Metropolitan Detention Center on December 16. "I've got no alternative."

The 36-year-old artist has been behind bars ever since he was arrested in June 2002 for faking drawings by Jean-Michel Basquiat and sentenced to three years. But that has hardly affected his artistic productivity: The work he has made in the pen has been in four shows, including solo exhibitions in New York and Paris.

Still, prison authorities seem none too happy with their resident Art Star. Martinez has had work confiscated and was recently barred from the room where he has been making it. Hence this—his second—hunger strike.

Over six feet and 318 pounds at the time of his arrest, Martinez was once so broke that he slept in a container beside the Gowanus Canal. But he is also a sophisticated artist, a former assistant to the painter Donald Baechler and a curator of well-received shows (it was at one of these that he laid his mitts on the Basquiats he later copied). His own work was always interesting—it included hand-fabricated guns—but prison has taken it to a new level. He makes paper by mashing up books and greeting cards, and uses pen, pencil, and coffee grounds to draw his signature guns ("They don't much like my gun pieces here," he says) as well as portraits of fellow prisoners and a couple of unrelenting studies of his first hunger strike, which lasted 55 days and took him down to 185 pounds. With an eye to art history, he signs the pieces with both name and inmate number.

"The prison authorities are very aware of what's happening," says Ronald Sosinski of Chelsea's Proposition gallery, which mounted Martinez's most recent New York show this fall (his works sell for several thousand dollars apiece). "New York does not allow art in the prisons. It's the only state in the country that doesn't." Prison officials—who haven't returned calls—can't have been delighted that Martinez tried to get three new paintings to his gallery by labeling them as legal documents.

Some of Martinez's friends on the outside can be snarky, art-world-fashion, about his sweet-sour success. One sniped that the hunger strike might be just a punitive diet regimen. Certainly, as Martinez's privations increase, his career prospers. Among those who have acquired pieces are the designer Jean-Charles de Castelbajac and the Miami architect Juan Lezcano, who also owns work by Donald Judd. "I was overwhelmed," he says. "I bought two." A show is being discussed with the London magazine-cum-art gallery *Dazed & Confused*.

Two days before Christmas, John Eberenz, an artist and a friend of Martinez's, *did* get three works from him by mail. They are gun drawings, made with coffee grounds and jam. In an accompanying letter, Martinez said he was on the sixth day of his hunger strike. Since then, no one else has heard a word.

NEW YORK

JANUARY 12, 2004

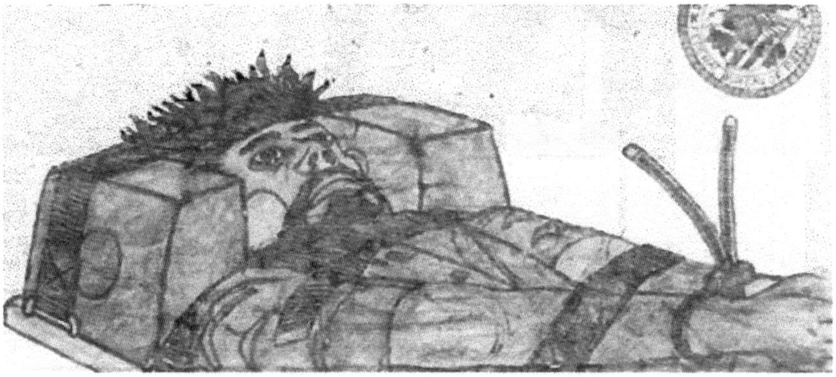

Why You Fucking with my Boy Picaso?
The Saga of Alfredo Martinez countinues...

by James Fuentes

Convicted art forger, Alfredo Martinez, corresponds with old friend and curator, James Fuentes, about his experiences in federal prison.

Since my previous article was published on Alfredo Martinez and his Basquiat forgeries, I have reestablished contact with him. Most striking to me is that even in federal prison, he continues to do what he loves most: draw. Despite his criminal past and the controversy surrounding it, his primary interest is still in making a career for himself as an artist. I have written the following account with the help of letters and telephone conversations I've had with Alfredo Martinez.

\- - - -

So there I was, drawing away. I made about 15 drawings. I would have made more, but the inmates kept bugging me to make drawings for them, and I would draw portraits of inmates and their girlfriends or some silly cartoon they wanted to send their kids. The inmates would want to pay me for the drawings, but I would not let them. "Why would I want the canned fish they sell here? It smells like cat food."

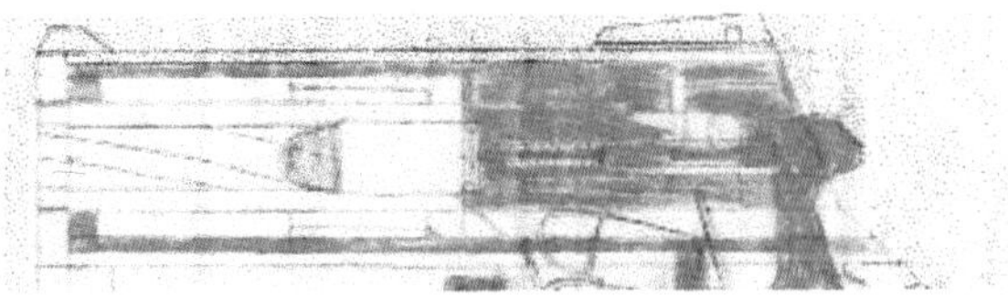

I would get up at 6 AM to line up for breakfast, milk and prison-made cake. Then, in the TV room, I would make paper by gluing scraps of blank paper with a glue mix I make with bread and water (a trick I learned from a Russian inmate friend of mine). When the paper was big enough and dry (that would take a day), I would glue on to it the back page of a magazine or paper from a book to make it thicker. With some paper ready, I would draw all day long, stopping only for lunch at 11 AM and dinner at 5 PM. Then I'd work until 11 PM when they turn off the lights.

Until the 19th of August, I had no trouble. On that Sunday, Safety Inspector Engram happened to see what I was working on in the TV room (a drawing of a .50 caliber sniper rifle). He walked over and asked what this was all about. I told him I was making drawings because I was trying to organize a show of my artwork. He asked if he could take a drawing to show someone. So, I let him take one, kept on working and forgot about the incident.

A week later, after lights out, a guard called my name. Everyone began to hoot and holler. I got out of my bunk and met up with a guard named Bregose; a one-time member of the NYPD, but not a bad guy. (Actually none of the guards are; they're just overworked.) Bregose demanded that the other inmates "Shut the fuck up!" and then informed me nervously, "Lieutenant Bledsoe from S.I.S. wants to see you." The room broke into long ooohs and catcalls. "He's going to the hole!"

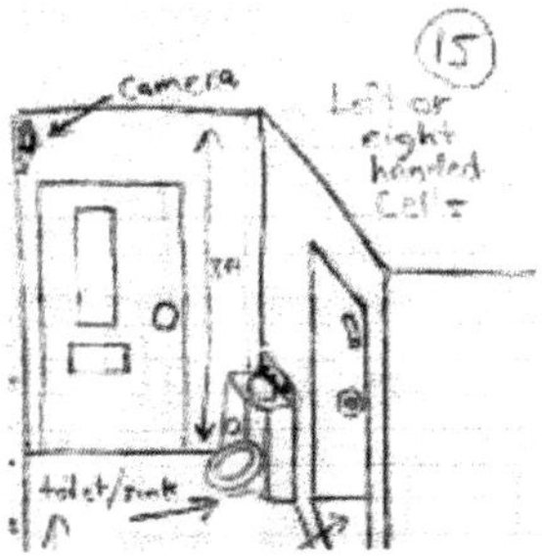

As we walked to the door I asked, "What's this all about," to which he replied, "I don't know." He gave me a sad look and added that he was "sorry." Even the guards don't like the S.I.S.; it's like the Gestapo here.

Safety Inspector Services investigates both

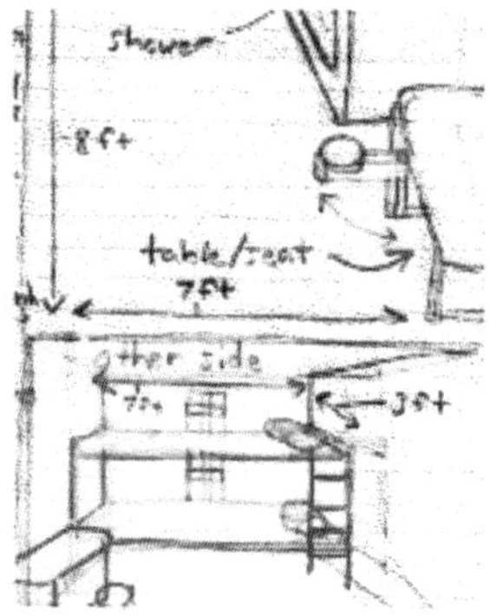

guards and the inmates. The officer I was going to meet was Lt. Bledsoe, head of the S.I.S. As I entered the hallway, I saw three more guards. One asked me if I could please put my hands up against the wall so that he could search me. Then I was told to wait. I squatted on the floor waiting for a little while. One of the guards shouted, "Bledsoe's here!" as he came down to our part of the hall. I didn't bother to get up.

Bledsoe is a tall, thin man of about 50 years with an olive complexion and black hair, cut in a sharp crew cut. He wore the same uniform as the other guards: a white short sleeved shirt with a B.O.P. patch on his right arm, a name and rank tag on his right-hand pocket, gray pants, heavy shoes, and a police-type belt with all of the police-type gadgets. But no gun. Guards only carry their guns (9mm Ruger P95) when they're outside. Oh, and one last detail: he had a short Hitler mustache. I kid you not!

Without looking at me, Bledsoe asked, "Is that Martinez?" With a nod, he crouched down beside me and said, "I came back from vacation to find this in my mailbox," to which I replied, "So that's where my drawing went! I was wondering what happened to it!" He threw the drawings at my feet and stared at me for a moment.

Martinez: What's the problem officer?
Bledsoe: So this is yours?
Martinez: Yes, of course.
Bledsoe: What is this? And where do you get the paper?
Martinez: That's my artwork and I was making them for art shows here in New York and in Europe. The paper I made out of paper they give me here using bread or oatmeal and water as glue.
Bledsoe: You have more?
Martinez: Yes, I get up at 6 AM and work all day.
Bledsoe: Go and get them.
So I stood up and went to my locker, fetching my drawings amid more hoots and hollers. I then took them to the hallway where Bledsoe was waiting.
Bledsoe: Is this all of them?
Martinez: Yes, I think so.
He looked at them all over as I unrolled them and laid the drawings flat.
Bledsoe: Are you in a gang?
Martinez: No. I don't think they allow art forgers in gangs.

Bledsoe: What are you in here for?

Martinez: Art forgery. You can look at my legal work if you want to.

Bledsoe: How were you going to get this all out of here?

Martinez: Fold it up and mail it out; I'm just waiting for money for stamps.

Bledsoe: We would never let you mail this out.

Martinez: Why not? I've been doing this out in the open for the last month and a half and there is nothing about what kinds of art you can do around here in the rulebook.

Bledsoe: Where's the book with the .50 caliber sniper rifle you drew?

Martinez: I don't need a book. I draw from memory. I'm a gun expert. This is what I would draw on the outside. I've been reviewed in the New York Times.

Bledsoe: Are you a terrorist? Other inmates may find what you do offensive and attack you.

Martinez: All the other inmates want me to do is draw pictures of their girlfriends and cartoons for their kids.

Bledsoe: Where do you steal the paint?

Martinez: The colors come from come from the coffee, tea or juice that all the inmates get here.

Bledsoe: I'm afraid you'll have to wait until you get to the outside before you can make any of this again. Get this man out of my sight.

As I was led back to my bunk, fellow inmates asked me what happened. "They took my drawings." "Man that's fucked up!" Since it was late and most of the inmates were awakened by the commotion, they started shouting, "Fuck you," in Spanish and English, and throwing raspberries, making fart noises, and asking "Why you fuckin' with my boy Picasso?" The commotion came to an immediate halt when three guards charged in and yelled, "Who wants to go to the hole?" Bledsoe rushed behind one the guards and whispered something into his ear—and then the guard called my name. When I approached him, the guard told me I would be searched again, handcuffed and taken to the hole. The whole place went nuts. Men were screaming and throwing things.

Bledsoe: I'm taking him to the S.H.U. (a.k.a. the Special Housing Unit or "the hole" by inmates; known to most as solitary confinement). When I get back, I want a full shakedown of this unit.

A shakedown is a group punishment in which all the inmates are moved to a common space and individual rooms are thoroughly searched. Big plastic carts are rolled throughout the unit to collect contraband. Contraband includes weapons and drugs, but mostly it consists of food and clothes. Technically, you can't have food or clothes that aren't issued by the jail.

Bledsoe turned the unit inside out in a severe shakedown that lasted until 4 AM—searching mainly for books about guns. He left each cell a mess and removed all the microwaves and a television. He was furious that he didn't find anything. Afterward, I was led through a maze of hallways and elevators that were remarkably similar to the video games I like to play (Metal Gear Solid, Doom, Quake.)

When we finally got to the door of the S.H.U., Bledsoe called on his radio, "Bledsoe on your Cheryl door." The door buzzed open and he handed me to a guard who took off my handcuffs and put me in a cell for a strip search. First I took off all my clothes—tan jump suit, t-shirt, underwear, socks. Then I was asked to run my hands through my hair, pull my ears back, open my mouth and stick out my tongue, show him my hands, turn around and show the bottom of my feet. And then, everyone's favorite: squat and spread my ass cheeks. They gave me an orange jumpsuit and told me to get dressed. I was moved to the cell where I have spent a lot of time since that incident.
An inmate can find himself in the S.H.U. for all sorts of reasons: fighting, contraband, investigation for his own protection, and sometimes, if there is no room for him anywhere else. I found myself there for "Investigation for Terrorism."

You are kept in your cell 23 hours a day. For one hour each day, you can go on the roof deck for an hour. It's an area about 10 x 25 feet with a heavy metal grate on top. Inmates stand around, talk, and smoke homemade cigarettes out of tea. Meals come through a plastic slot in the door. Lights go on at 6 AM and off at 11 PM. Even though you're on the top floor, there is no view. The windows are fogged with acid. Below I have drawn a view of the S.H.U. cell from the top bunk.

James Fuentes is an independant curator living in NY

Alfredo Martinez " Heckler & Koch P7-13" 2002

(drawn from memory) pencil on paper 8 _" x 11"

Courtesy James Fuentes

Alfredo Martinez " Special Housing Unit" (detail)

pencil on paper 8 _" x 11"

Courtesy James Fuentes

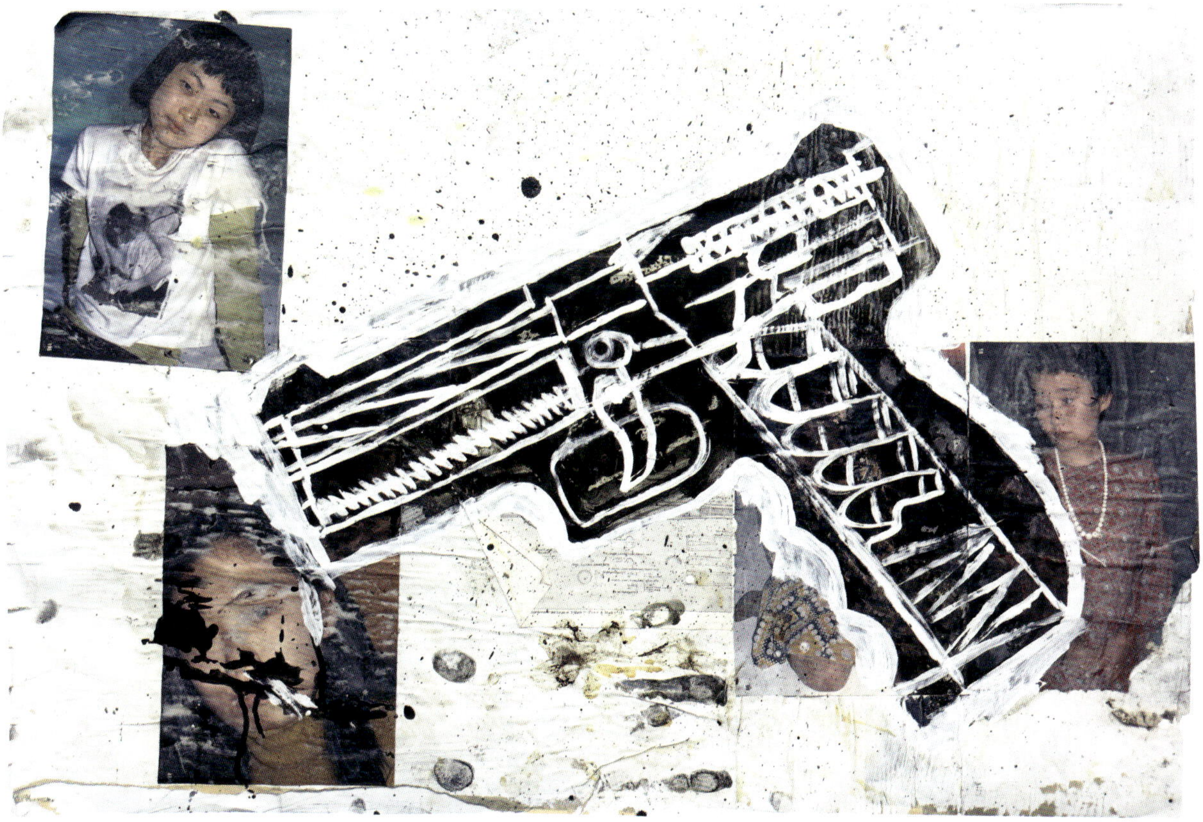

Asia Porn

1999

Mixed Media on Hand Collaged Paper

24 x 36 in.

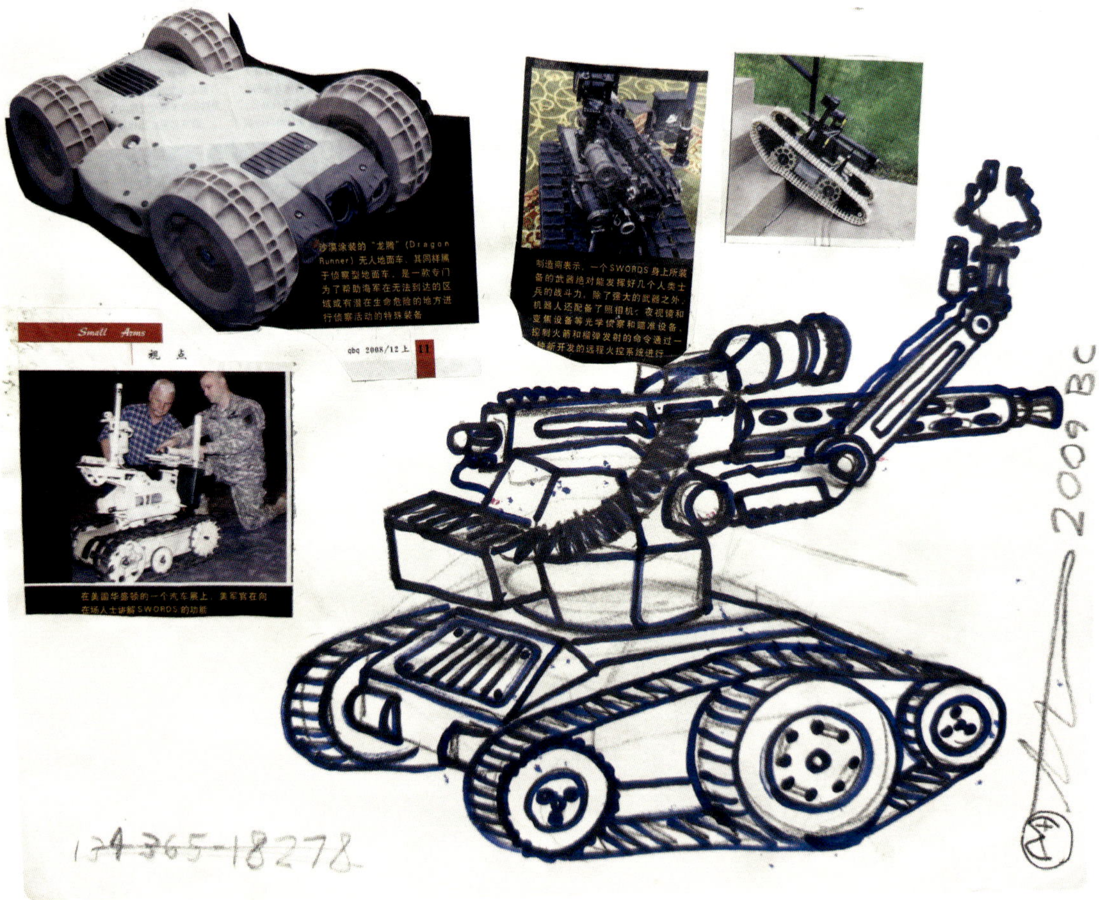

Notebook Drawing #4

2009

Mixed Media on Hand Collaged Paper

11 x 14 in.

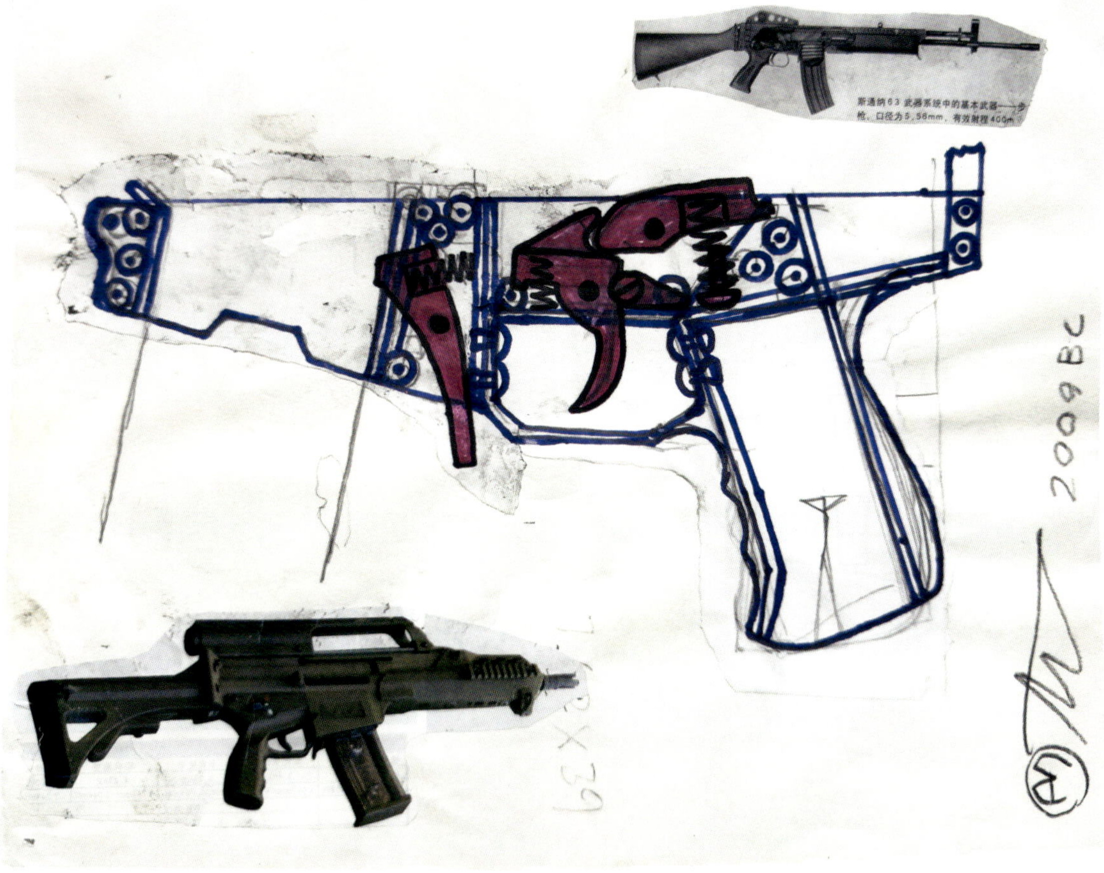

Notebook Drawing #5

2009

Mixed Media on Hand Collaged Paper

11 x 14 in.

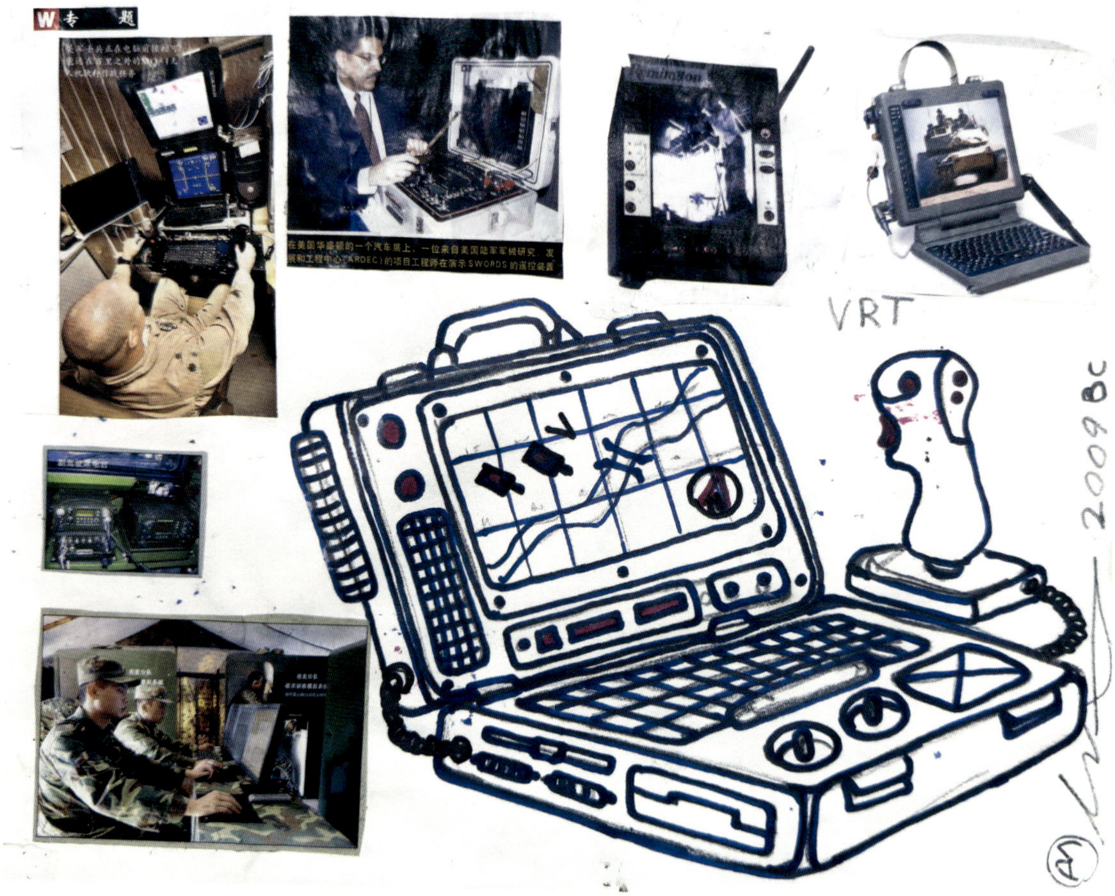

Notebook Drawing #4

2009

Mixed Media on Hand Collaged Paper

11 x 14 in.

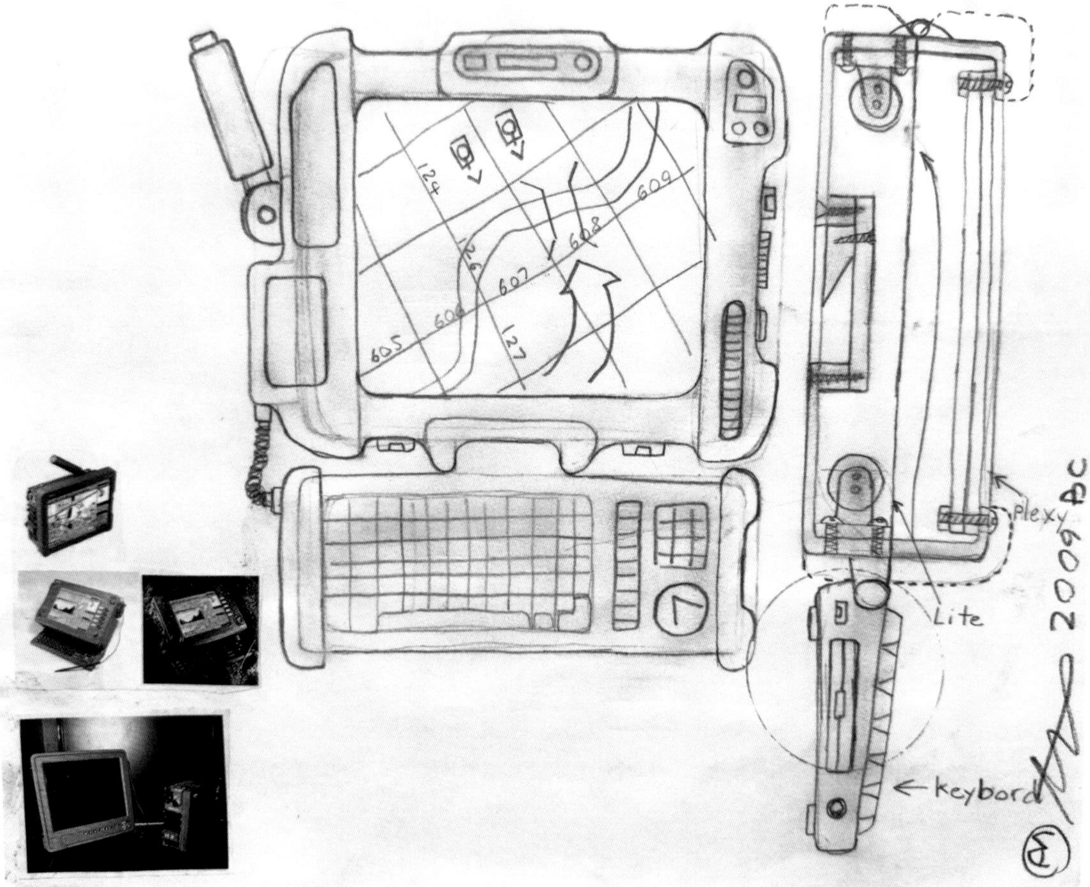

Notebook Drawing #5

2009

Mixed Media on Hand Collaged Paper

11 x 14 in.

THE ADV
A VA

by Marc Hungerbuhler

My relationship with Alfredo has unfolded over decades within the shifting terrain of the New York art world, alternating between moments of intimacy and turbulence, and others of relative quiet. We first encountered one another at Exit Art in the 1990s, initiating a sustained exchange of exhibitions in which our roles alternated: at times he curated my work, and at others I included his practice within my own curatorial frameworks. From the outset, Alfredo revealed a singular sensibility for discovering and presenting artists who were, at that moment, largely unknown but who would soon emerge as central figures within the metabolism of contemporary New York art. His exhibitions—frequently staged in unconventional venues such as derelict storefronts, artists' studios, or other marginal spaces—resisted institutional conformity while generating unexpected currents across artistic, social, and cultural boundaries. In doing so, he expanded prevailing definitions of artistic medium and demonstrated a rare capacity for dissemination that marked his practice as both generative and destabilizing.

As an omnipresent figure in the downtown scene, Alfredo became a social and artistic nexus. Nearly everyone who encountered him carried a vivid memory or anecdote—whether voiced with admiration, irritation, or outright condemnation. He circulated seamlessly between diverse cultural life strata, forging connections ranging from international celebrities such as David Bowie and Julian Schnabel to critics, writers, and the inner circles of New York's artistic establishment. His radical approach to artmaking, compounded by equally uncompromising lifestyle choices, made him both an object of fascination and the sub-

ENT OF NISHING

ject of mythologies that oscillated between reverence and scandal.

More than an artist, Alfredo is an embodiment of art itself. He has long inhabited a paradoxical position: at once a careerist of immense ambition and a figure prone to self-destruction, depression, and nihilism. His tendency toward self-sabotage might be read less as pathology than as a mode of renewal, a dialectical process by which he reclaimed the psychic energies necessary to sustain his prodigious creativity. Over the years, Alfredo has been a collaborator, co-conspirator, interlocutor, and gatekeeper in New York and China. Together, we pursued projects that bordered on the impossible, yet his presence also served as an anchor for communities of artists working at the margins of dominant cultural institutions. Like a gravitational field, his influence was never entirely absent; it ebbed and receded, only to return with renewed force, demanding resilience from those within his orbit.

Financial precarity has been a constant in his life. When in possession of money, Alfredo tended to disperse it rather than retain it. My own collection of his drawings and prints has grown mainly through these cycles, each work arriving in moments when he appeared at my door seeking support, leaving behind another fragment of his oeuvre.

It is difficult to recall an exhibition I have curated in which Alfredo Martinez was not a central presence. The extraordinary exertions required and the inevitable drama that accompanied his participation often yielded outcomes that exceeded the sum of their parts. At times, however, the completion of work was foregone and only the drama remained.

From Rikers to Beijing

Following Alfredo's widely publicized incarceration for wire fraud and subsequent fifty—five—day hunger strike at Rikers Penitentiary, the Artist Network was approached by the District Attorney's office with an unusual request. They proposed that Alfredo, still under parole and residing in a halfway house, be integrated into our organization through a formal sponsorship arrangement. It was a pragmatic and redemptive gesture: a means of facilitating his reintegration into society while allowing him to channel his creative drive into structured, communal work.

Within our lower Manhattan space, Alfredo assumed various roles—coordinator, curator, and custodian—each undertaken with his characteristic blend of fervor and improvisation. He oversaw day-to-day operations, collaborated with staff, and contributed decisively to the formation of our curatorial program. His influence extended across many initiatives: the Art Kids program, internships, international residencies, and exhibitions that carried his unmistakable imprint. Over time, he became a permanent fixture within the organization's fabric, inhabiting the space almost as an extension of himself. I often found him on my office floor early in the morning, needing a broom, mop, and shower, necessary to maintain a professional environment.

It was during this period that our discussions began to turn outward. We contemplated establishing a new base in Mexico City to expand our residency and exhibition programs. Yet our trajectory shifted unexpectedly when we received an invitation from Mr. Zhao Shulin, director and chief curator of the Imperial Museum in Beijing. The introduction came through the Chinese artist O Zhang, who had encountered our work and spoke of it during her travels. In 2006, Alexandra—my wife and co-director of the Artist Network—and I accepted Zhao's invitation and journeyed to Beijing. We discovered a city in the throes of cultural transformation: the Beijing art world radiated an energy that was raw, entrepreneurial, and utterly compelling. It was immediately clear that our next chapter would unfold not in Mexico City but in China.

From that point forward, our attention turned fully toward Beijing. The first major initiative, Surge, was conceived for the 798 Arts Festival in the summer of 2007. The exhibition brought together twenty artists from Spain, Switzerland, Mexico, Germany, Ireland, Poland, Sweden, the United States, China, and Finland—marking the Artist Network's inaugural presence on Chinese soil. Alfredo had been deeply involved in the preparatory stages in New York and regarded Surge as his opportunity to reassert himself within an international arena. His participation, however, remained uncertain, hampered by his legal restrictions and lack of funds. Through sustained effort and negotiation, we obtained special authorization from the District Attorney's office permitting him to travel abroad. Ronald Sosinski of Proposition Gallery generously provided the financial means to make the journey possible.

For Alfredo, Surge represented far more than an exhibition; it was a reclamation of self—a chance to project his creative spirit beyond the confines of New York and the shadow of his past.

In the spring of 2007, Alfredo arrived in Beijing. The city was suspended between eras, its vast expanses of demolition and construction evoking both ruin and promise, a fitting landscape for an artist perpetually negotiating between collapse and renewal.

Huang Yan and the Surge

Huang Yan, the conceptual artist, entrepreneur, and gallerist, extended a generous invitation, offering the Artist Network a temporary home within one of his art compounds near the Seventh Ring Road, not far from the burgeoning 798 Dashanzi Arts District. There, among a labyrinth of half-converted industrial buildings, he provided studios and living quarters for our international residents, including Swiss artists, some of the earliest participants from our clients, the Merian Foundation.

For Alfredo, Beijing proved to be extraordinarily fertile ground. The art world was in the midst of an awakening—eager to engage with foreign artists, hungry for exchange, and unburdened by the bureaucratic formalities that often-constricted Western institutions. The cost of living was minimal, the sense of possibility immense. With his inimitable combination of brilliance, irreverence, and charisma, Alfredo navigated this new terrain with instinctive precision. Within weeks, he had insinuated himself into the very center of Beijing's cultural metabolism. Journalists like Stacey Duff and Tom Pattison from Time Out, diplomats, curators, collectors, and artists alike were captivated by his presence; his name circulated through the district with intrigue and admiration.

He was omnipresent in the 798 scene. No internet café, restaurant, or studio was beyond his reach. At Time Zone 8—a bookstore and café owned by Robert Bernell that functioned as an informal agora for artists and theorists—Alfredo bartered drawings for sustenance, exchanging a week's worth of sandwiches for quick portraits scrawled on the spot. There was something almost performative about this survival economy, an alchemy through which necessity became art.

The Surge exhibition unfolded within an unfinished FedEx warehouse—a cavernous ruin of concrete pillars bristling with rebar, its ceiling leaking in viscous streams pooling into shallow basins on the floor. Sand mounds and debris occupied what might have been the exhibition hall, half-constructed staircases led to nowhere, and the absence of electricity or sanitation lent the site an air of desolate grandeur. It reminded me of a post-apocalyptic cityscape—less an art venue than a landscape awaiting resurrection. The logistical challenges were immense. When Alfredo first surveyed the site, his eyes lit with delight. He turned to me and declared, "It's perfect! Can I live here?" To which I replied, without hesitation, "Of course."

Alfredo soon relocated to the Surge site, inhabiting the derelict warehouse as though it were both studio and stage. Our small crew had assembled a team of security guards—a rough but reliable group tasked with safeguarding the newly installed electrical lines, projectors, artworks, and other fragile evidence of civilization amidst the debris. They lived on-site, improvising a provisional community in the rubble, and for a time, coexistence unfolded with a strange harmony. Alfredo's disarming warmth and egalitarian spirit bridged language and class with ease; he treated the guards as equals, fellow laborers in constructing a dream. Yet such an equilibrium was fragile. It faltered when Alfredo, confused notions of socialist camaraderie with appropriation, began to help himself to their food supplies.

One afternoon, amid the exhibition, a small delegation of officials appeared at the warehouse.

Their sudden presence—the gleaming Land Rovers idling at the gate, the uniformed escorts stationed nearby—introduced an aura of bureaucratic theatre to our post-industrial ruin. When I was called to the site, Alfredo greeted me with characteristic nonchalance, presenting the officials as old friends. Through our translator, I learned they represented a new development initiative: an arts district in Hegezhuang, further east of Dashanzi. They were eager to enlist us for an inaugural cultural event that would lend credibility and international cachet to their enterprise.

Sensing an opportunity, Alfredo assumed the role of diplomat. He spoke with conviction about the virtues of open competition, artistic exchange, and the necessity of transparent collaboration—a deft improvisation that, as always, merged sincerity with performance. Within moments, the officials had invited us to inspect their facilities, and we found ourselves whisked away in a convoy of Land Rovers toward Hegezhuang.

After a half-hour journey through Beijing's expanding outskirts, we arrived at a sprawling complex under construction: vast halls of concrete and steel, their skeletons suggesting future museums and galleries of monumental scale. The site they proposed for our next exhibition was an airplane hangar—immense enough, they boasted, to house four 747s. We disembarked at a set of administrative buildings where additional officials awaited our arrival. The atmosphere here was markedly different from the anarchic, commercial bustle of 798. Hegezhuang exuded a sense of order, perhaps even quiet authority; uniformed guards patrolled the premises with military posture.

As we traversed the corridors of the main building, we entered a grand meeting room adorned with flags representing nearly every nation. I thought it had the surreal aspect of a geopolitical stage—a United Nations of Art in China. The ensuing discussions were lengthy and ceremonious, circling themes of cultural diplomacy and the soft power of art. Hours passed; the room filled with cigarette smoke and the clinking of teacups. Finally, as daylight faded, our hosts declared it was time for dinner—an indispensable ritual in Chinese negotiations, where conviviality often sealed the terms that contracts would later formalize.

We were escorted through a manicured park, past lotus ponds and sculpted hedges, until we reached a traditional pavilion set gracefully upon a lake. The setting was breathtaking and cinematic. Guards saluted as we passed, the solemn gesture bordering on the absurd. There, beneath the lacquered eaves, an elaborate meal unfolded: two perfectly grilled sirloin steaks, countless side dishes, plum wine poured in endless rotation, and a round of Cognac to close the evening.

By its conclusion, the agreement had been reached. Alfredo—ever adaptable, ever persuasive—had accepted their invitation to curate the Chinese counterpart to Surge, featuring a selection of local artists. I, in turn, committed to relocating the second installment of the project to Hegezhuang once the 798 exhibition concluded. As we prepared to depart, Alfredo, with his familiar blend of charm and audacity, turned to Mr. Li, the district's director, and asked if he might move in immediately to begin preparations. Mr. Li smiled and replied, "Of course."

Alfredo had finally found a new home away from the Surge security guards—and a patron eager to indulge his every whim. The months of relentless labor at 798, the sleepless nights spent fortifying the Surge site against the elements, the bruising negotiations, and the endless improvisations had, it seemed, culminated in this improbable triumph. In Hegezhuang, Alfredo stood at the center of the whirlwind he had helped conjure.

The transformation was startling when I returned a week later after consulting with our participating artists. The site itself appeared to have grown, as if inflated by ambition. Two guards stood at the gate, greeting Alfredo with crisp military salutes. He emerged from within—clean-shaven, freshly shorn, attired in a white dress-shirt, a heavy Rolex glinting on his wrist. He moved through the space with the assurance of command, issuing instructions to workers and assistants, though directing a small army. Inside the compound, the atmosphere was electric: young hires at computers fielded calls and typed incessantly, scaffolding rattled against steel beams, and the drone of machinery blended with the shouts of foremen. It had the feel of a nascent institution—less a warehouse now than a museum in the making, with Alfredo as its self-appointed director.

What followed was pure Alfredo: an unrelenting surge of energy that bordered on the manic. He conducted what must have been a hundred studio visits a week, bursting with ideas, provocations, and boundless charm. Within weeks, truckloads of artwork began arriving; cranes and crews labored day and night to raise walls, hang lighting, and assemble the impossible. The exhibition—aptly titled Dream Palace—brought together more than fifty Chinese and international artists and formally inaugurated the 2,700-acre complex that aspired to rival Dashanzi's 798 as Beijing's new cultural capital. The event was less a vernissage on the opening night than a coronation. The Dream Palace became legend.

Zhou Shulin

Among the figures who shaped our Beijing trajectory, none loomed larger than Zhou Shulin—the omnipresent and formidable curator-director of the Imperial Museum of the Forbidden City. He first extended the invitation that drew me to Beijing in 2006, and through him, I entered the intricate networks of the Chinese art establishment, particularly those converging in the 798 complex.

Shulin possessed an instinctive fascination with Alfredo. Yet he viewed the A-Space initiative with suspicion. Its principal backers—Mr. Li and the elusive Mr. U.H. Lee, financiers of the Dream Palace project, occupied a sphere of influence at odds with his own. Their rivalry, grounded in subtle political antagonisms, made the project a point of quiet contention. Even so, my relationship with Shulin endured. I had introduced him to Alfredo, sensing a shared affinity: both were larger-than-life figures, drawn to spectacle, power, and seduction. Each possessed a capacity for deception so artful it verged on performance.

Shulin was a man of immense resources and rare erudition. His background was as improbable as impressive—educated in Eastern Europe, trained in military diplomacy, and later returning to Beijing as an expert in the nuanced theater of "soft power." He held high-ranking positions in governmental and private cultural institutions, navigating tensions with a tactician's finesse. I often found myself in his company at meetings whose gravity I did not fully grasp—encounters with officials whose authority seemed to extend beyond art, and from which I was never sure I would safely return. Shulin was drawn to Alfredo's audacity, stories, and dangerous magnetism. In exchange for support and access, Alfredo would regale him with tales that hovered between truth and delirium—accounts of Lio Malca, the FBI, the Feds, and shadowy operations that seemed to collapse myth and memory into one. Inevitably, their alliance took on the cadence of mutual fascination and latent distrust.

Shulin summoned me again, commissioning a curatorial intervention for the Bridge Art Museum in the newly developed SoHo Beijing Art District. His request came with a curious stipulation: I not only "manage" one of his artists—Alfredo Martinez—but also oversee the installation of a full-scale replica of an assault helicopter as part of the museum's opening event. And so, inevitably, Alfredo re-entered the narrative, returning from the mythic glow of Dream Palace into the volatile orbit of Shulin's domain.

I often wondered whether Alfredo, in his characteristic manner, had finally overplayed his hand. Perhaps he had met his match in Shulin—a man who could mirror his charisma, absorb his cunning, and anticipate his every move. Whatever the case, the promised rewards of this alliance never fully materialized.

Afterward, I relocated Alfredo to a space I had been developing—Huang Yan's HYCAC Beijing 1 (Huang Yan Contemporary Art Center). Within the compound stood a modest residential house, and Huang, ever generous, allowed Alfredo to stay there. I hoped a new project might restore his morale and revive his creative spirit. We planned an exhibition titled Critical Mass, which we would co-curate—a venture that, I imagined, could bind together art and survival in equal measure.

But Alfredo had changed. The fire that had once propelled him now seemed dimmed. Demoralized after the Bridge project, he drifted through the compound with diminished purpose, avoiding meetings and declining to engage. During this desolate period, he received an invitation from the Jamaican Ambassador to attend a reception at the Hilton in Chaoyang. Ever impulsive, Alfredo set out alone on a small moped—an absurd vehicle for his 300-pound frame. Somewhere along the route, he lost control and crashed along a major thoroughfare.

The Embassy's account of his arrival bordered on the surreal. Bloodied and limping, he entered the soirée like a wounded apparition, collapsing just inside the door. Embassy staff quickly retrieved his mangled scooter, transporting both man and machine back to HYCAC, where the Ambassador's physician tended to him with alarming urgency. But Alfredo's condition soon worsened. Our mutual friend Jeff Gompertz, who had been with us since the earliest days in Beijing, became his caretaker—feeding him, cleaning his wounds, and monitoring his fever. Still, Alfredo refused all medical help. His wound began to fester; the air in his room grew heavy with decay.

Then, as suddenly as he had appeared, he vanished. One morning, he was simply gone—no note, no trace, no word of where he might have gone or who might have aided him.

Days later, as I sat at a noodle shop with several artists, preparing for the opening of Critical Mass, I glimpsed a familiar figure passing behind the translucent windowpane. The silhouette was unmistakable. I leapt to my feet, rushed into the street, and shouted his name. He turned, slowly. His eyes were half-shut, his face hollow, his clothes filthy. He looked spectral—like a ghost walking through daylight, a man dislodged from his life. I guided him back to the restaurant in stunned silence. Around us, conversation ceased. Alfredo sat there, trembling, muttering incoherently about indelible and unfathomable things. It was clear that he had reached the end of something—a breaking point beyond art, beyond recovery.

In 2008, as I was completing the construction of a studio and residential complex in Caochangdi for our international residency clients, one of our German artists, Martin Wehmer, informed me that Alfredo was back in 798. He was alive.

My family and I were preparing to return to New York after two years in Beijing so that our children could re-enter public school in the U.S. We were also organizing what would become our most ambitious project in China — the Beijing 798 Biennial. The original curatorial director, Zhu Qi, from the 2007 798 Arts Festival, had approached me to curate the following year's edition. Still, I persuaded him to reimagine it as a biennial — an expanded platform integrating commercial and non-commercial spaces across the district.

It was an immense endeavor, requiring the assembly of an international network of artists, curators, and sponsors, as well as delicate negotiations with corporate and private partners. For nearly a year, I commuted between New York and Beijing, managing the logistics of this large-scale initiative. During that entire period, I neither saw nor heard from Alfredo.

When we finally arrived in China for the installation and opening of the Biennial, he appeared — as if out of thin air. He attended the events and moved among the artists and guests, but had no work to show; communication had long since broken down. After the Biennial closed, Alfredo vanished once more. Though I returned to Beijing frequently in subsequent years, our paths never crossed again.

Nearly a decade later, in 2017, while I was in New York developing a longlist for the Havana Biennial in Cuba, I learned that Alfredo had also returned to the city. I reached out. We met. The idea of collaboration emerged effortlessly, as it often had. We planned to bring twenty international artists to Havana, Alfredo as co-curators and participants. Yet, the entire effort unraveled just as the Cuban Commission approved our project. Shifting U.S.–Cuba relations and the political uncertainty surrounding Raúl Castro's departure abruptly ended our sponsorships.

When I returned from Switzerland in 2023, I received the devastating news of Alfredo's passing. Perhaps naively, I had hoped that we might one day reconcile the unfinished chapter of the 2009 Beijing Biennial. Like so many of our shared ambitions, that reunion was not meant to be.

The Return

After our return to New York, we rarely spoke about the alleged incident in China that led to Alfredo's arrest. His accounts of what had transpired were vivid and cinematic—descriptions so elaborate they left little to the imagination. His storytelling always had a performative quality, as though he were drafting the script of a film in which he was both protagonist and unreliable narrator.

In his apartment, he left drawings scattered across every surface: tables crowded with half-finished soda bottles, empty take-out containers, stacks of magazines, and laundry half-buried under sheets of paper glistening with fresh paint. The place resembled a hybrid between a studio and a set—disorder elevated into mise-en-scène.

Given that his serviced apartment included weekly cleaning, it is not difficult to imagine the staff's shock upon entering. Confronted with Alfredo's meticulous blueprints of firearms and explosive devices—sketched with architectural precision—they must have imagined themselves standing inside the lair of a would-be terrorist rather than the workshop of an artist. Panic, inevitably, ensued. Police were called. And what followed, by Alfredo's telling, unfolded with the ambiguity of a Rashomon-like narrative—multiple realities layered one atop another, each alternating between the plausible and the absurd.

According to him, his arrest had cascaded through several tiers of authority: first local police, then homeland security, and finally ICE, once he was repatriated to the United States. Whether entirely actual or filtered through his penchant for theatrical embellishment, the episode fit seamlessly into the larger mythology of his life. It reaffirmed his identity as provocateur and victim of circumstance—a man whose artistic and criminal legacies had long been intertwined.

In retrospect, the story seemed too coherent, too symbolically aligned. In uncanny resonance, it echoed the similar detention of Ai Weiwei in 2011—a parallel Alfredo himself no doubt appreciated. For him, the incident in Beijing completed a perfect circle: the outlaw artist confronting the machinery of the state, the individual subsumed into the spectacle of control. It was, in its own way, his most performative work—unintended, yet perfectly in character.

Epilogue: The Distance Between Us

There are certain people whose gravity never releases you, no matter how far you drift. Alfredo was one of those rare souls whose orbit remained constant, even when time, geography, and circumstance conspired to pull us apart. Our paths separated for years—different cities, different urgencies—but the current between us never truly quieted. It ran beneath the noise, beneath the surfaces of art and ambition, beneath the failures and improbable recoveries that marked our lives.

We were competitive like siblings drawn to the same fault line—the volatile intersection of art and survival, creation and self-undoing. Where I sought structure, Alfredo sought rupture; where I built, he dismantled. He gave motion to what I sought to frame, and I offered form to what he risked dissolving.

There were times I needed distance from him, and times he

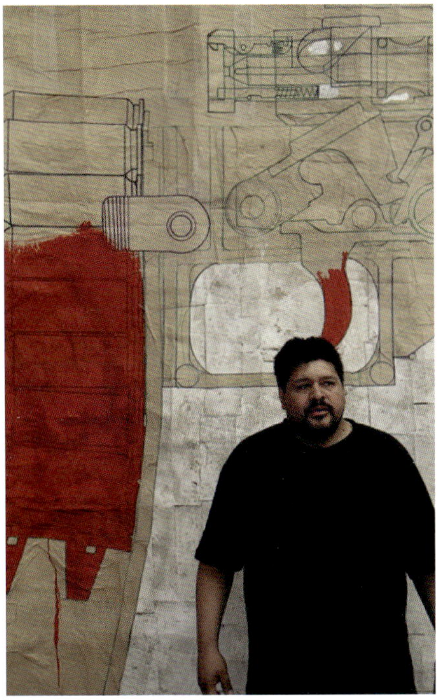

fled from me. But distance, I understood, is not absence—it is a different way of staying connected. Even when continents lay between us, our dialogue continued in other registers: through rumor, memory, and unfinished work that outlived its making. We would vanish from each other's orbit only to reappear again—New York, Beijing, Havana—as if no time had passed, as if the conversation had merely paused mid-sentence.

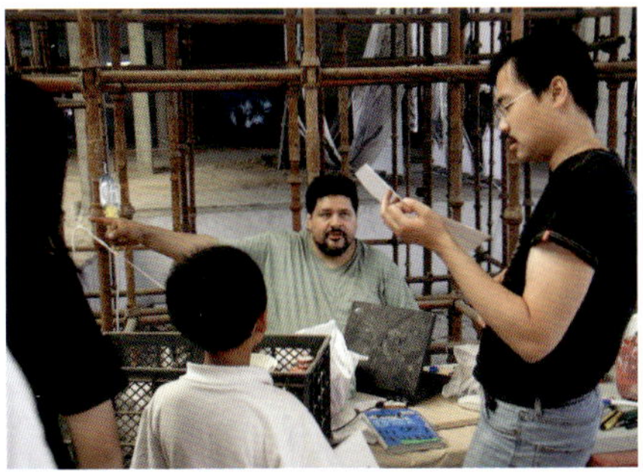

Alfredo inhabited contradiction with disarming honesty. His life oscillated between brilliance and collapse, generosity and chaos. He tested every boundary—moral, social, legal—not to destroy them but to challenge what lay beyond their fragile authority. Beneath his bravado lived an acute sensitivity. He could read a situation or a person with startling precision. When stripped of illusion, he understood that beauty often revealed its most human form in failure and destruction.

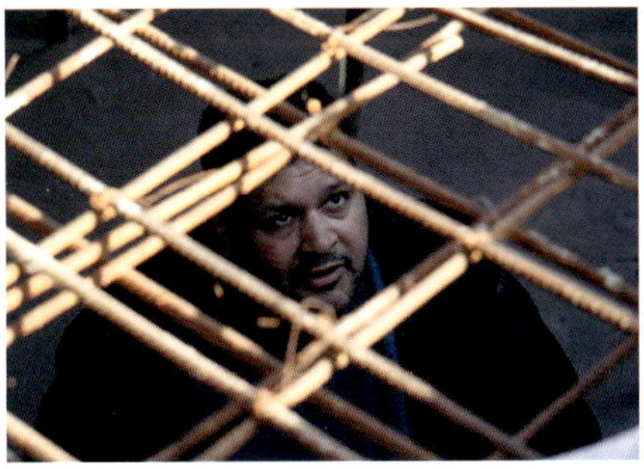

Our story was never about achievement or legacy. It was about endurance. Art was not a career, but a condition; not a means of control, but a way of remaining alive to the world's unpredictable pulse.

In the end, what remains are not the exhibitions or the archives, but the traces of shared time—moments suspended between crisis and creation, between audacity and surrender, between the real and the imagined. Alfredo taught me that chaos, too, has symmetry, and that even the unfinished carries its own perfection.

And so, our conversation continues—now without words, across a distance no longer measurable in space or years, but only in memory.

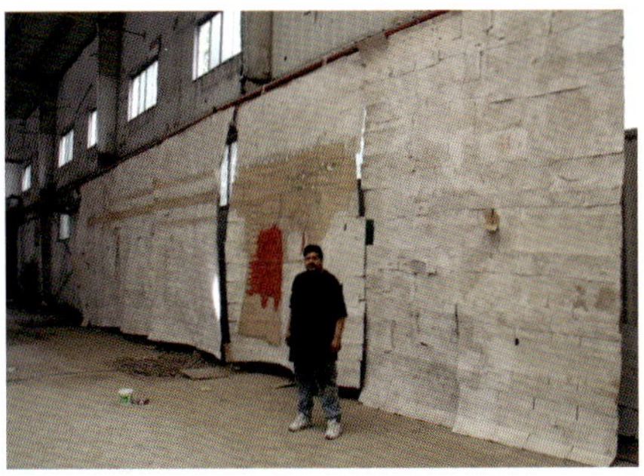

Marc Hungerbuhler New York, Monday, October 13, 2025

Disclaimer: *"This memoir is a truthful recollection of actual events in the author's life. While the stories in this book are true, some names and identifying details have been changed to protect the privacy of the people involved. Some conversations and events have also been recreated and/or supplemented based on the author's memory, which is imperfect."*

ALFREDO MARTINEZ: New Work After China February 24 – April 9, 2011

Posted on January 28, 2011 | Leave a comment

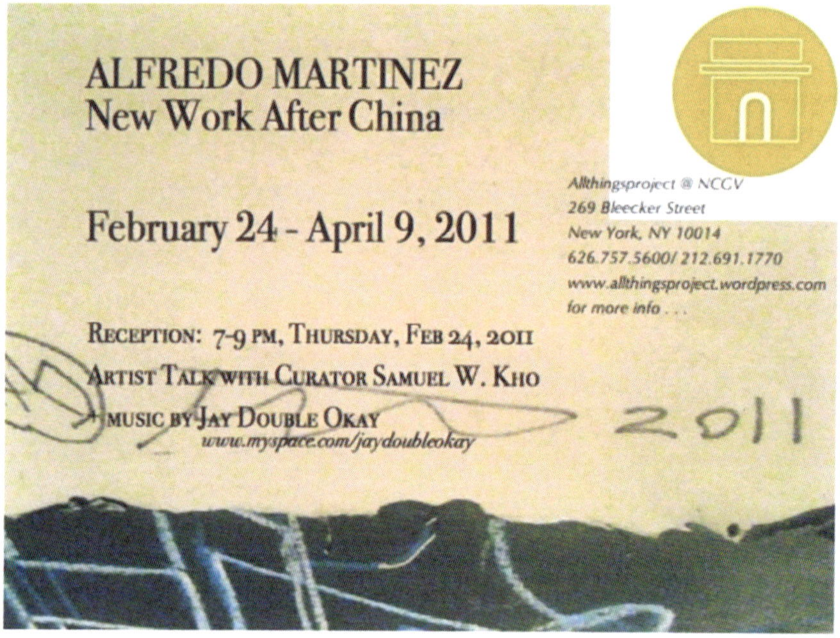

"He shall judge between the nations, and rebuke many people; they shall beat their swords into plowshares . . . Nation shall not lift up sword against nation, neither shall they learn war anymore." (Book of Isaiah 2:4)

"Beat your plowshares into swords
And your pruning hooks into spears;
Let the weak say, 'I am strong.' " (Book of Joel 3:10)

Allthingsproject is pleased to present a solo exhibition with **Alfredo Martinez**, the first after his three-year experience in China. Martinez was missing the ol' "True Grit" of New York City, and so he went to work overseas. He brought back homey tales, such as of donkeys carrying coal in Beijing streets, but he also barely escaped, after three weeks of harrowing detainment by their secret police. His friends include those in the highest levels of China's cultural elite; but true to form, his recent travails supersede his previous, news-making incarceration for forging Basquiats.

Of course, his dearest subject matter remains the Gun. Alfredo Martinez may just be the Jules Winnfield ("And I will strike down upon thee with great vengeance . . .") in the Pulp Fiction of the contemporary art world. Martinez the artist-philosopher and d-i-y weapons master holds the rationale for why the gunslinger steps out of retirement, or what forces the hand of the everyday farmer, or where the ethics could be in aesthetics. His drawings of weaponry are emblematic of present society: efficient, potent, lethal. Irrationality cannot simply be displaced with modern rationality, but rather, finds salvation in prophecies of when Chronos is visited by the Kairos of God– that one day, weapons of war could be elegaic, composed shards viewed only in museums. Then and only then, old soldiers retire for good.

A Timeline About the Artist

1967– Raised in Sunset Park, Brooklyn, and Pennsylvania

1989– After time working in Central America, joins US Army, plays loanshark to soldiers; also stations in Europe

1994– Involved in both East Village art and LES hardcore punk scenes; included in Pat Hearn Gallery's "Skater Angels"; works for arms dealer in Paris, polishing weapons knowledge

1999– Included in PS1's "Generation Z" exhibition; had been weapons advisor for Jim Jarmusch's Ghost Dog (1999) and Henry Bean's The Believer (2001); Creates and supervises active shooting range for 'Quiet', produced by Josh Harris and Leo Koenig, documented within Ondi Timoner's We Live in Public (2009)

2002-2004– Arrest by FBI and jail for Basquiat-related art forgery. Hunger strikes in prison returns his art-making privileges. Works assembled in one-man show at The Proposition gallery in Chelsea.

2005– Included in MoMA's Judith Rothschild Foundation Contemporary Drawings Collection; also Hello Kitty 30th Anniversary, Mori Art Center, Tokyo, Japan

2007-2010– Lives and works in Beijing, China; interrogation and detainment over three weeks before being deported back to United States

2009– We Live in Public wins Best Documentary at Sundance Festival

2010– Exhibits at White Box, SCOPE Miami

ALFREDO MARTINEZ: New Work After China is the first exhibition of Allthingsproject in 2011, the third year of exhibitions organized by curator Samuel Kho. The curatorial appointment is made possible by a generous grant from the Mustard Seed Foundation, matched by individual gifts. Allthingsproject and its gallery are part of the Neighborhood Church of Greenwich Village (NCGV), a house of worship that unabashedly supports cutting-edge visual practices, thoughtful lectures, as well as music and spoken word performances. More info at www.allthingsproject.wordpress.com and www.ncgv.net.

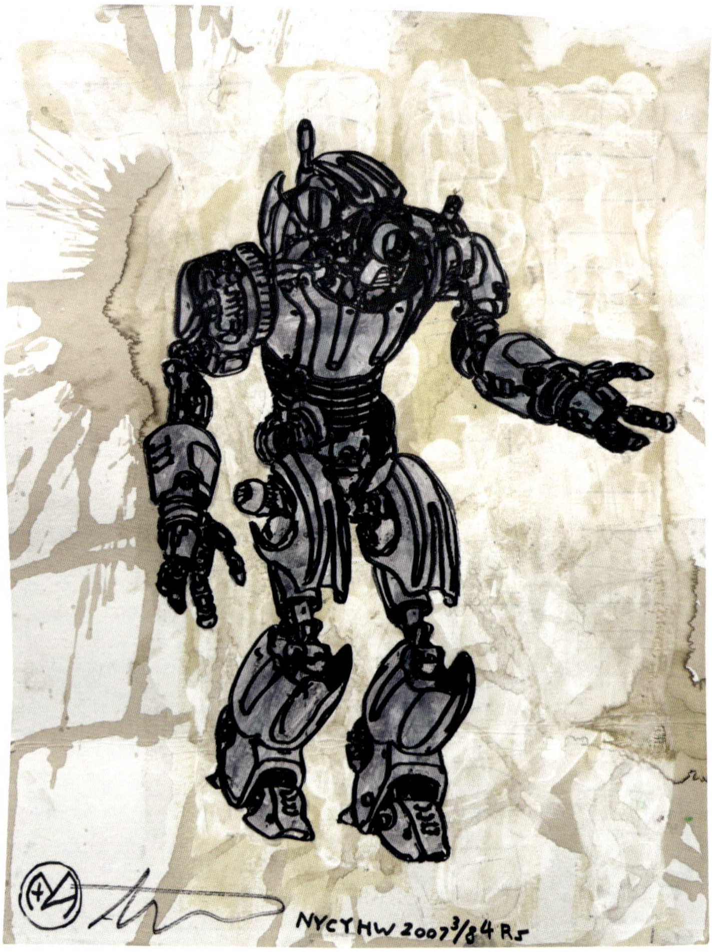

Robot Drawing #1

2007

Mixed Media on Hand Collaged Paper

22 x 28 in.

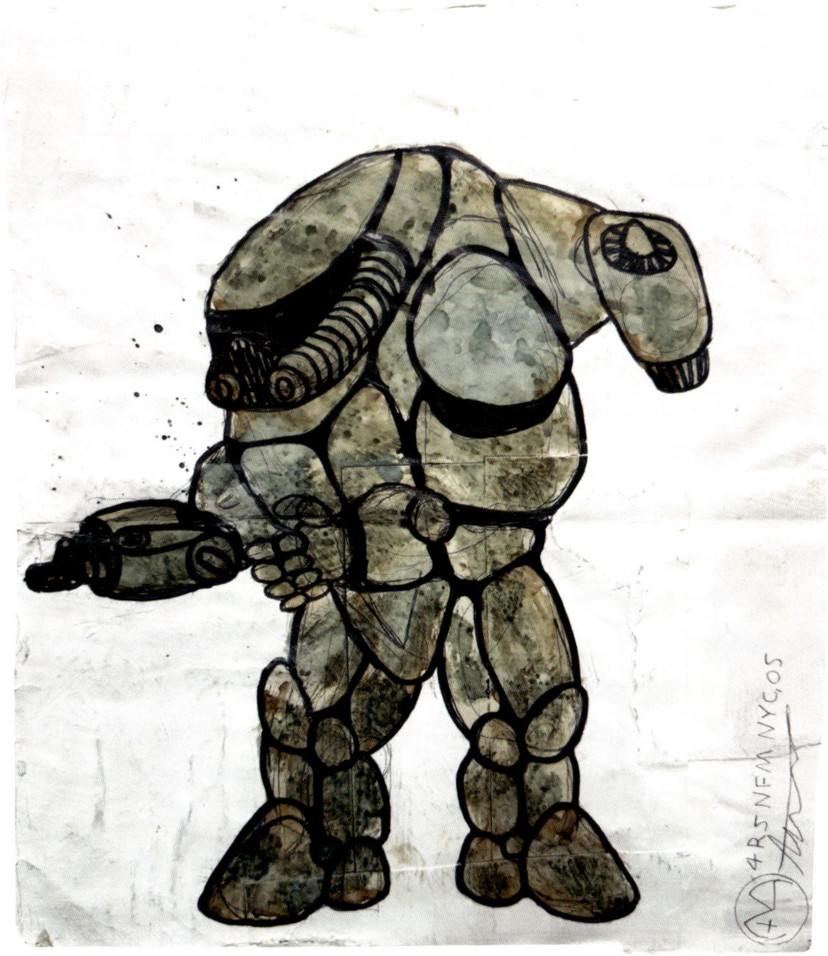

Robot Drawing #2

2007

Mixed Media on Hand Collaged Paper

16.5 x 14.5 in.

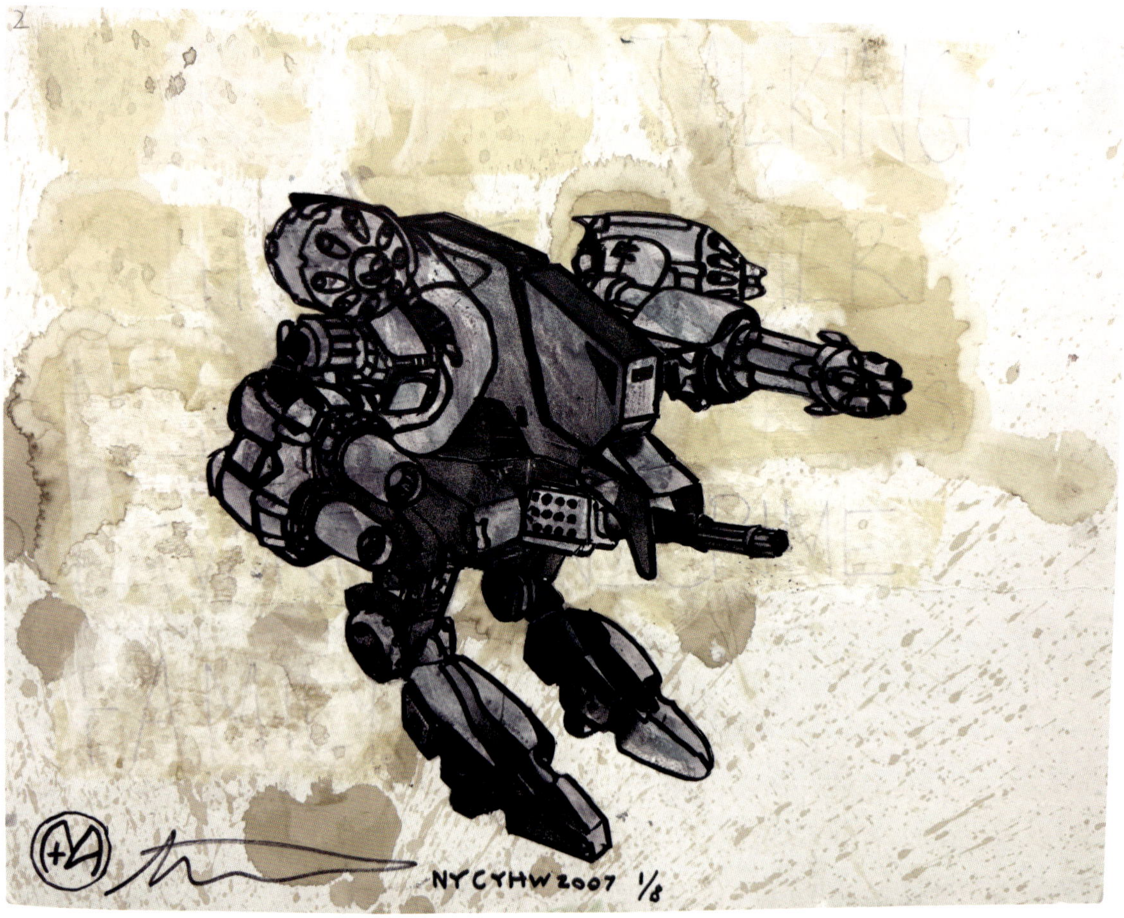

Robot Drawing #3

2007

Mixed Media on Hand Collaged Paper

22 x 28 in.

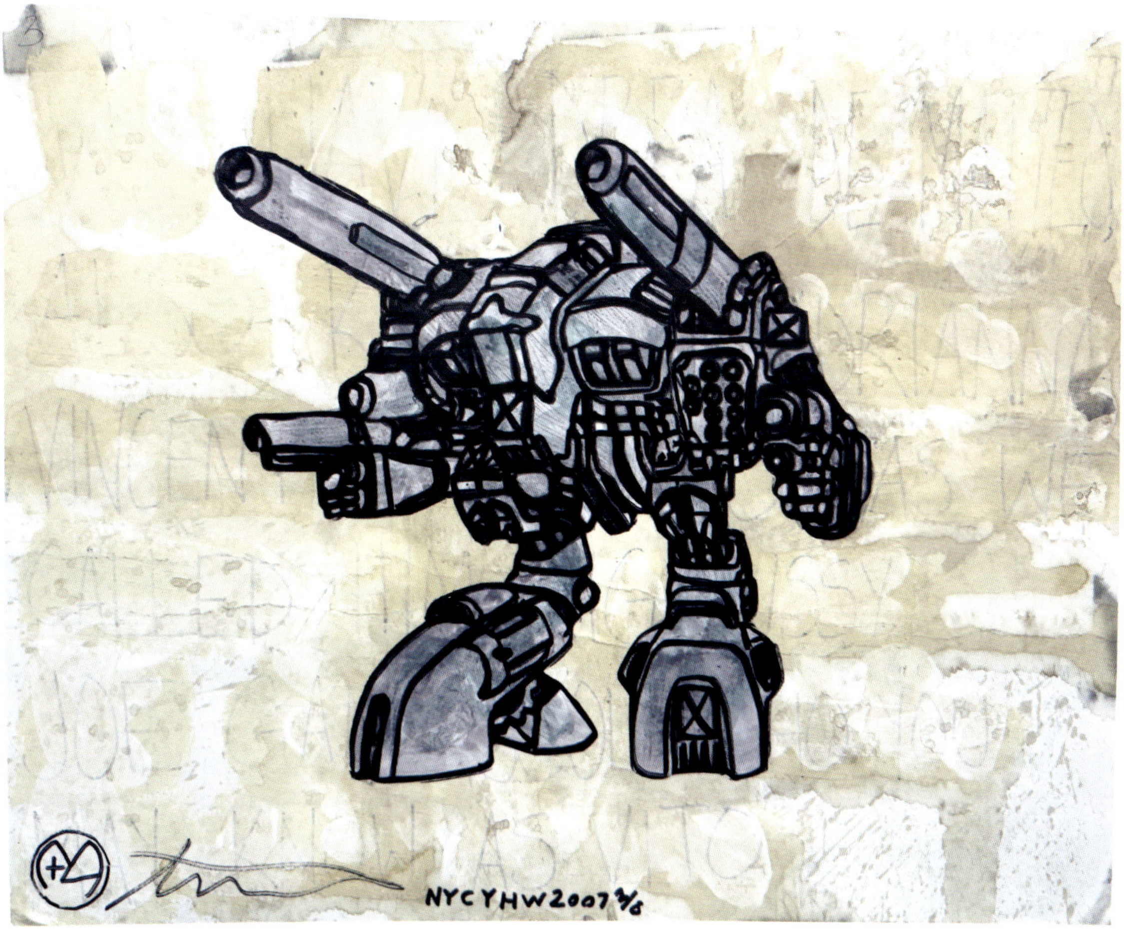

Robot Drawing #4
2007
Mixed Media on Hand Collaged Paper
22 x 28 in.

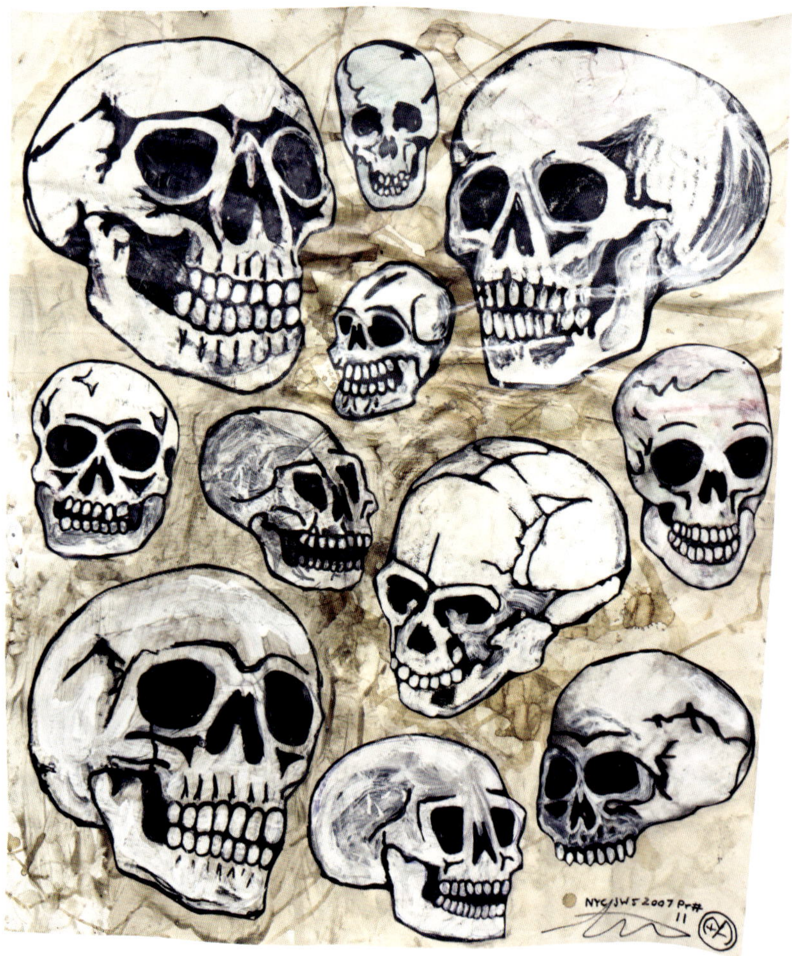

Skull Drawing #1

2007

Mixed Media on Hand Collaged Paper

38 x 32 in.

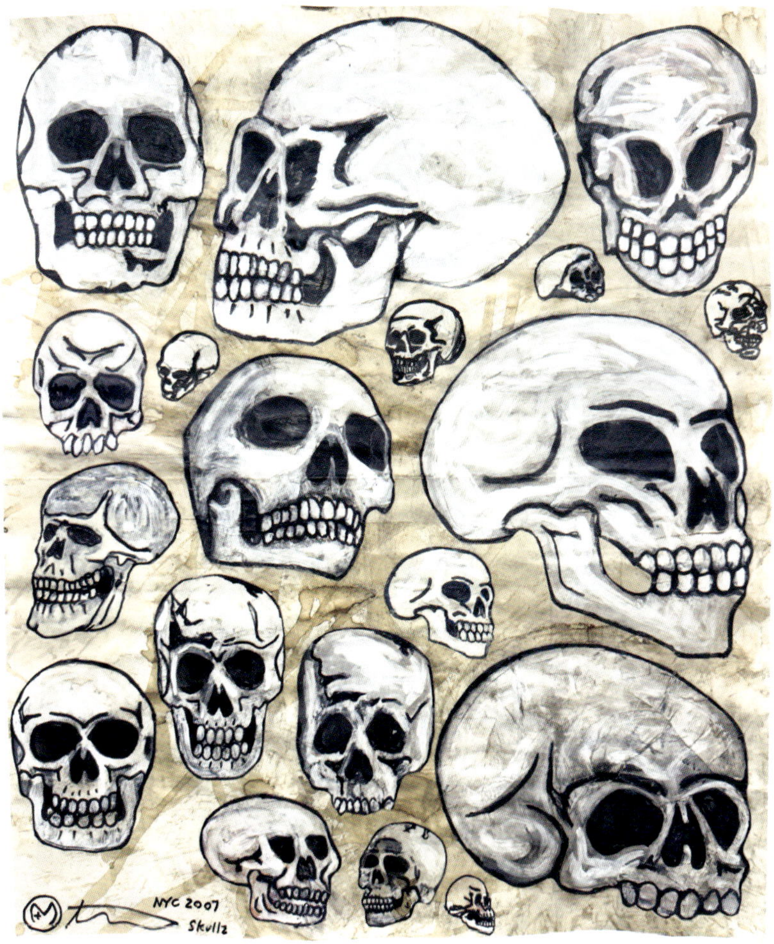

Skull Drawing #2

2007

Mixed Media on Hand Collaged Paper

38 x 32 in.

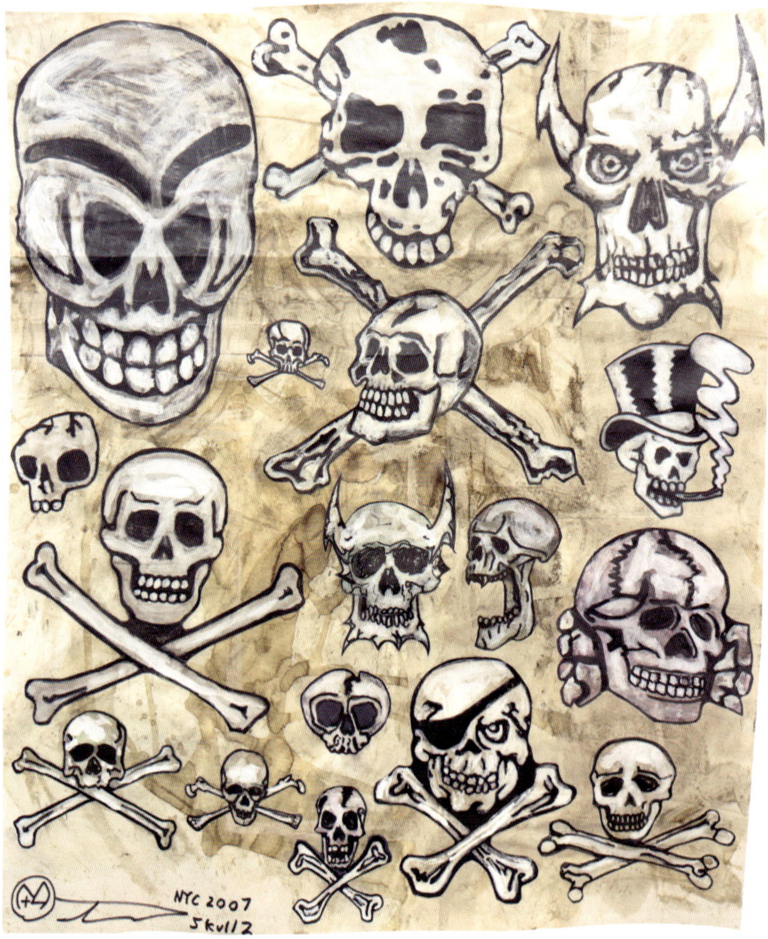

Skull Drawing #3

2007

Mixed Media on Hand Collaged Paper

38 x 32 in.

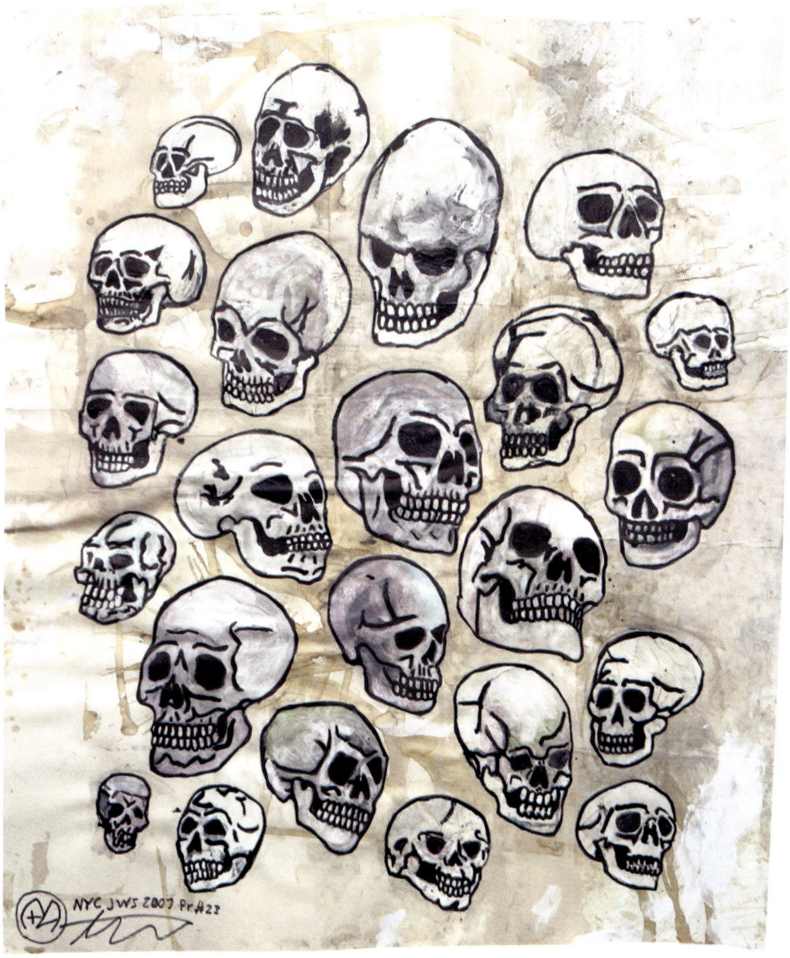

Skull Drawing #4

2007

Mixed Media on Hand Collaged Paper

37 x 32 in.

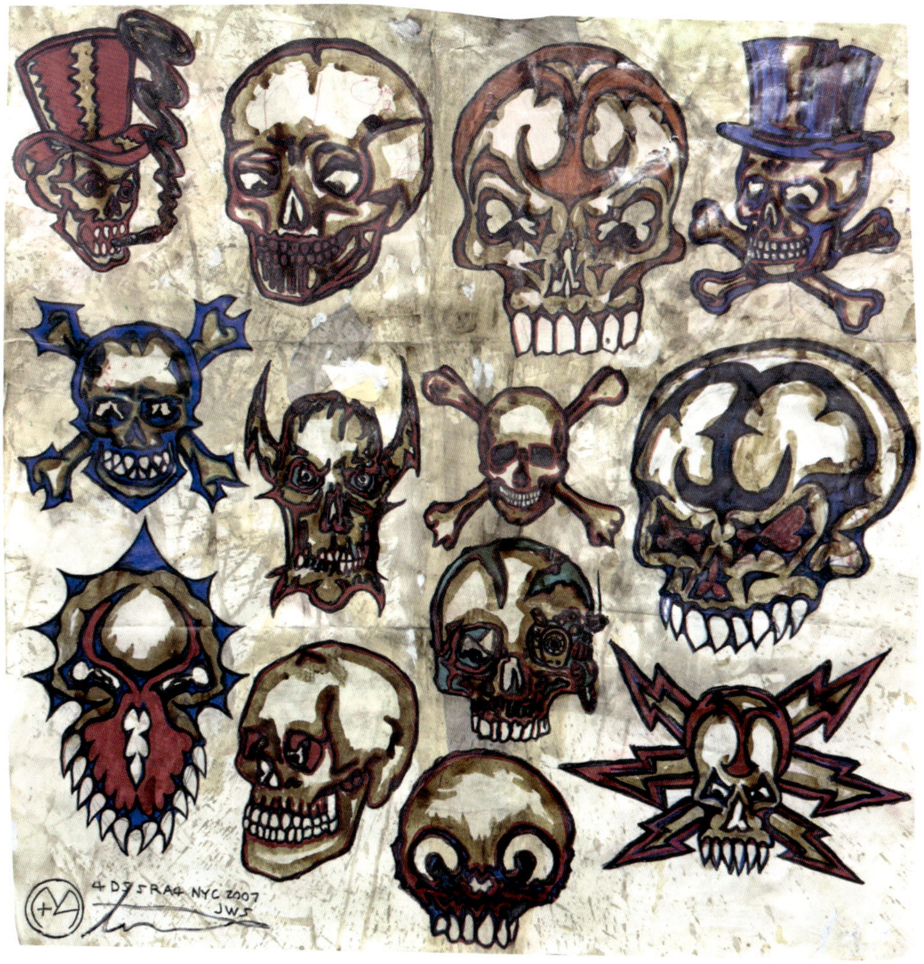

Mixed Skull Drawing

2007

Mixed Media on Hand Collaged Paper

33 x 32 in.

The New York Times https://www.nytimes.com/2023/09/11/obituaries/alfredo-martinez-dead.html

Alfredo Martinez, Who Fused Art World and Underworld, Dies at 56

He created hoopla around art made in prison — first in the early 2000s, with himself as the artist, then 20 years later with the scammer Anna Sorokin.

By Alex Traub

Sept. 11, 2023

Alfredo Martinez lived on New York City's margins, a squatter who shook off one eviction after another. He was an artist who usually lacked a gallery and sometimes put on exhibits in a storage locker.

Yet Mr. Martinez was also a player in the world capital of culture and media.

He mastered a few artistic techniques. He had the chutzpah to break the rules. He saw that criminality could be a neighbor of fame. And he talked in the colorful manner that makes journalists listen.

Mr. Martinez synthesized those qualities into an idiosyncratic strategy as a bohemian provocateur: Use prison to supercharge an art career.

He did that in the early 2000s, after he pleaded guilty to art forgery. And with his guidance, Anna Sorokin transformed herself from a celebrity scammer being held in an immigration detention facility into an artist selling pencil and acrylic drawings for $10,000 a pop.

It was one of many ways Mr. Martinez brought together New York's art world and underworld.

He died on Aug. 21 at his home in Newark, where he had moved recently seeking space and stability, his brother, Javier, said. He was 56. Mr. Martinez had been treated for diabetes and an infection in his right leg that led to a series of amputations, beginning with his big toe and culminating above the knee.

Mr. Martinez's education in staging transgressive, carnivalesque art spectacles began when he was in his late 20s and 30s.

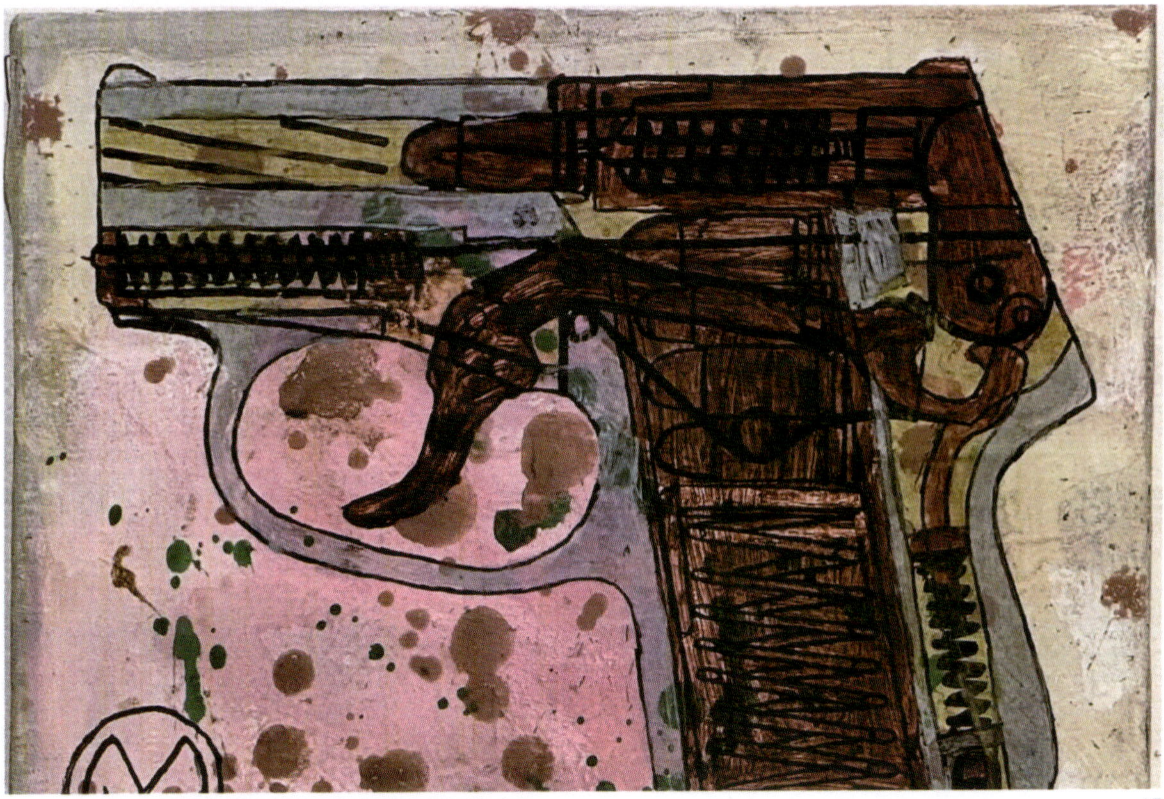

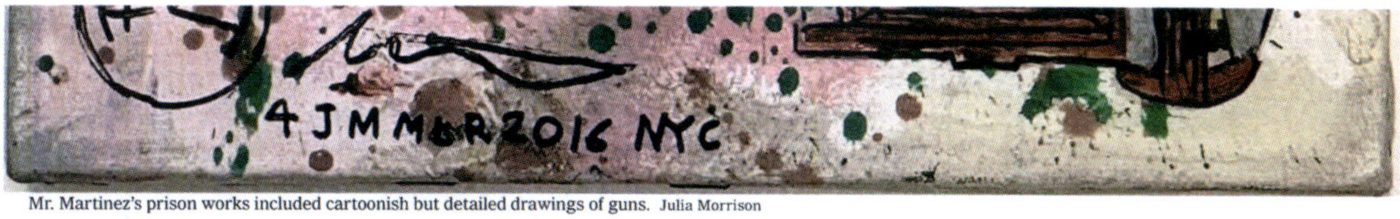

Mr. Martinez's prison works included cartoonish but detailed drawings of guns. Julia Morrison

In 1999, the tech mogul Josh Harris offered dozens of arty acquaintances a month's room and board in a downtown Manhattan bunker in exchange for the right to film everything they did. There was sex, drugs, military-style interrogations and, surreally, a well-stocked arsenal of guns and a shooting range. Mr. Martinez, credited as the "artillery artist," set that up. (His role in the project was later recorded in "We Live in Public," a documentary by Ondi Timoner.)

Around the same time, Mr. Martinez was curating group art shows, generally drawing work from artists he knew and using ersatz galleries that did not outlive the shows themselves. In 2000, one exhibit, "Na'er Do Wells," featured some unusually valuable objects: a drawing and a painted chair back by Jean-Michel Basquiat.

Basquiat's art gave Mr. Martinez an idea.

"I just knew instinctively it was something I could forge," he told The Village Voice in 2007. "It was such an easy way to make a quick 20 grand."

Using the Basquiats that appeared in "Na'er Do Wells" and their authentication papers as models, Mr. Martinez began a forgery operation. He sold two fake Basquiats to the New York art dealer Lio Malca, Artnet reported, and he approached two other dealers with offers.

In March 2021, while Ms. Sorokin was on parole, Page Six announced that "noted artist and curator Alfredo Martinez" had "fallen in love" with Ms. Sorokin's drawings.

Now Ms. Sorokin replied to Ms. Morrison and Mr. Martinez. The group began planning an exhibit.

Days after the Post article came out, Immigration and Customs Enforcement took Ms. Sorokin into custody for overstaying her visa. She faced the same difficulty that Mr. Martinez once had in making art while incarcerated. He came up with a solution: printing out images of her works and copying them, using the same tracing method with which he had forged Basquiat.

On March 17 last year — soon after the release of "Inventing Anna," a Netflix mini-series about Ms. Sorokin — a crowd of skateboarders, party people, curiosity seekers, contemporary art fans and journalists gathered in a shuttered downtown Manhattan storefront. It was a classic Alfredo Martinez group show and art spectacle.

"Free Anna Delvey!" the crowd chanted.

Ms. Sorokin called Mr. Martinez. He put her on speaker and held his phone aloft. Ms. Morrison told the crowd to shut up and listen.

Mr. Martinez smiled. Once again, he had New York's attention.

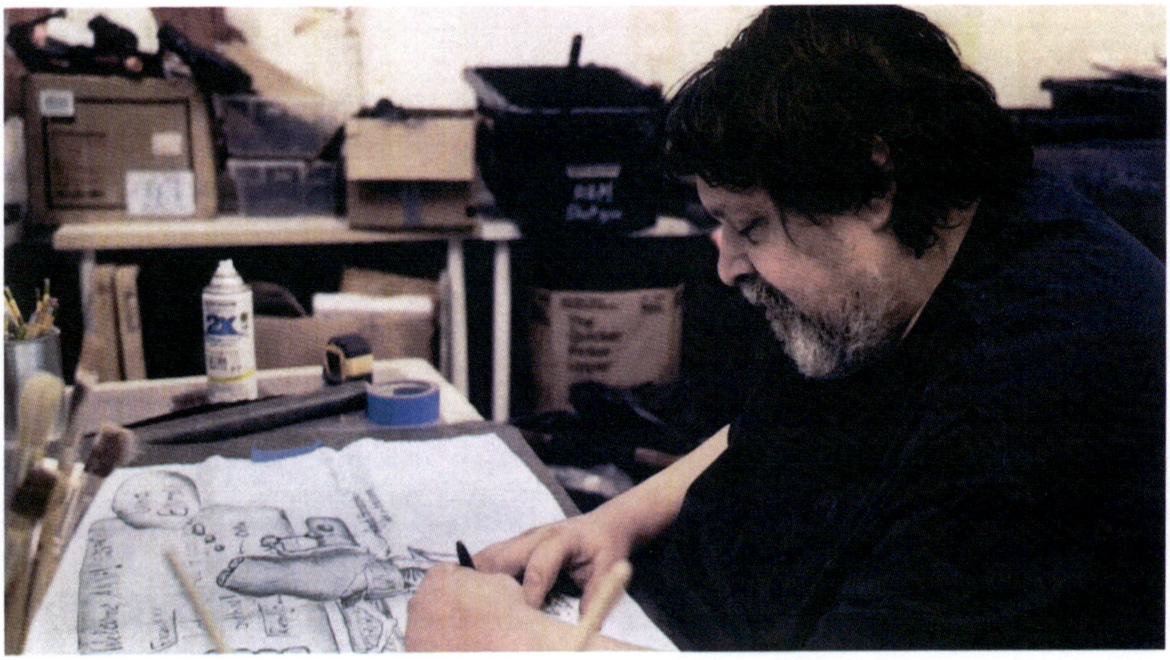

Mr. Martinez made art himself, exhibited works by others and had a forging operation. Julia Morrison and Quentin Pistol

Alfredo Martinez was born on April 15, 1967, in Brooklyn, to Alfredo and Sonia (Pereyra) Martinez. The family ran a junk store in Brooklyn, and they lived behind the store. Alfredo ran away from home as a teenager.

In addition to his brother, Mr. Martinez is survived by his father and two sisters, Sonia and Christine Martinez.

Some who followed Mr. Martinez's career called him a publicity hound. Curators asking around about him were advised to stay away. Even friends like Ms. Morrison often found themselves feeling exploited.

But it's not hard to find people eager to discuss not only Mr. Martinez's chicanery and showmanship, but also his artwork itself.

One of Mr. Martinez's preoccupations was making aluminum casts of pistols, revolvers and machine guns; it was among his techniques for using gun parts to create menacing yet toylike sculptures. In an interview, Mr. Haden-Guest called them "genuinely peculiar and unusual."

He added that Mr. Martinez might turn out to fit a familiar type: the troublemaker who posthumously gains renown as a serious artist.

"An artist with an unruly kind of life, a street life, who people find hard to accept in their lives — bang, when they're dead, they're there," he said. "They're part of art history."

Kirsten Noyes contributed research.

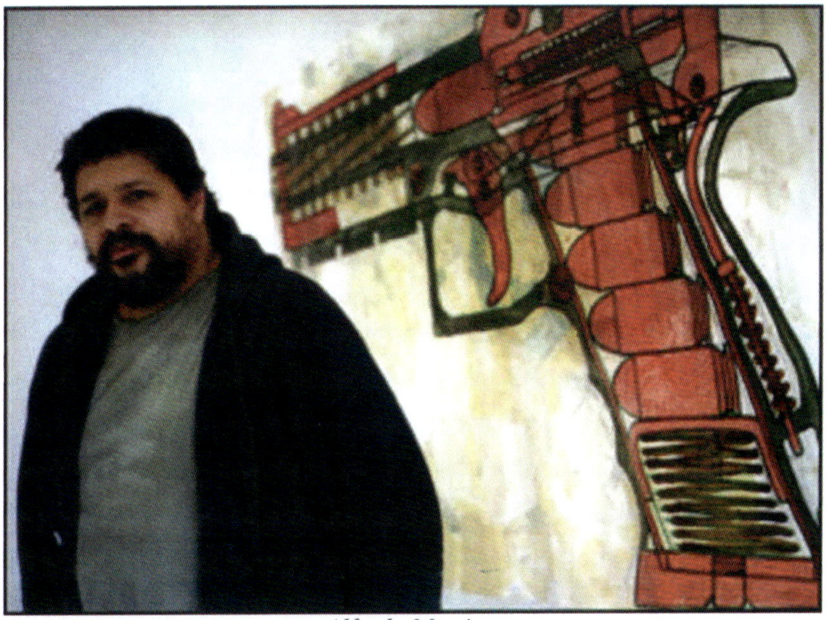

Alfredo Martinez

With an air of bemusement and wonder the first thing Alfredo Martinez said was, "You know, right when I think things are going to calm down, it's like it starts in all over again." That's taking understatement to new heights, considering he'd just been deported from China. It was September 2010 and Martinez had been back in New York for a couple of weeks, and though he didn't really look that worse for wear he did appear authentically shaken. The last time I had seen him was a year before in Beijing when we'd gone to an unnerving and bizarre Chinese Army shooting range where we were ushered into a large room with practically every type of gun and rifle in the world arranged on shelves behind glass. After being handed a "menu" of all the guns we checked off a few before heading over to the range where a completely normal Chinese family watched their daughter blast away. There's something disconcerting about a mousy teenage girl wearing a purple "KING" trucker hat wantonly firing a semi-automatic weapon. With a pistol and our battered AK-47 bolted to a school desk facing the range ("This one's a beater," according to Alfredo) we did a bunch of shooting. It was a really loud, kind of exciting, and somewhat nerve-wracking touristic diversion.

During the following year we had some intermittent contact, but in the summer of 2010 Alfredo seemed to drop off the map. In late August someone in Beijing who only knew Alfredo peripherally wrote asking if I'd heard anything, because it appeared Alfredo was missing and some people were worried. Up until then the lack of communication hadn't seemed like a reason to worry, but since this person wasn't a close confidante of Alfredo's his query suggested there was actually cause for concern. Then, three weeks later, guess who showed up in New York after being detained and exiled from his adopted homeland? On our second meeting (more on the first later), as is not out of the ordinary with Alfredo, before we got to the story of what went down there were a few digressions, like about that time he got shot in Guatemala.

"You know, in third world countries there are a lot of power outages, and I was in this big supermarket with off-duty soldiers as security. The power went out, and they made everyone come to the front of the store. We heard a car backfire and one of the soldiers freaked out a little bit and pulled the trigger on his rifle, it

That led to his arrest. Mr. Martinez pleaded guilty to wire fraud, according to Artnet, and was sentenced to more than two years in prison.

He saw the punishment as an opportunity. "Jail," he was fond of telling journalists in the years to come, "was a publicity stunt."

During his trial and imprisonment, he became a figure on gossipy Page Six of The New York Post. In October 2003, The Post reported, Mr. Martinez "managed to smuggle his jailhouse art — painted using coffee, Kool-Aid and fruit juice — to a Chelsea gallery" called the Proposition Gallery. The listed price of his works was $150,000.

In January the next year, the writer and art critic Anthony Haden-Guest reported in New York magazine that Mr. Martinez's work had appeared in four shows, including solo exhibitions in New York and Paris.

His prison works included cartoonish but detailed drawings of guns and a portrait of himself on a hunger strike strapped to a gurney preparing to be force-fed.

Many years after his release, Mr. Martinez was still trading on the glamour of his crime, introducing himself to a journalist from Insider by saying, "I'm a notorious art forger."

By then, he had found a new opportunity for his art-crime hucksterism.

In May 2020, Anna Sorokin was in the midst of a 4-to-12-year prison sentence for financial crimes. She had been the subject of magazine profiles, tabloid gossip and news coverage for posing as a German heiress named Anna Delvey and swindling banks, hotels and associates out of about $200,000. Now she had begun doing something new: having her friends post on Instagram self-portraits that she had drawn in prison.

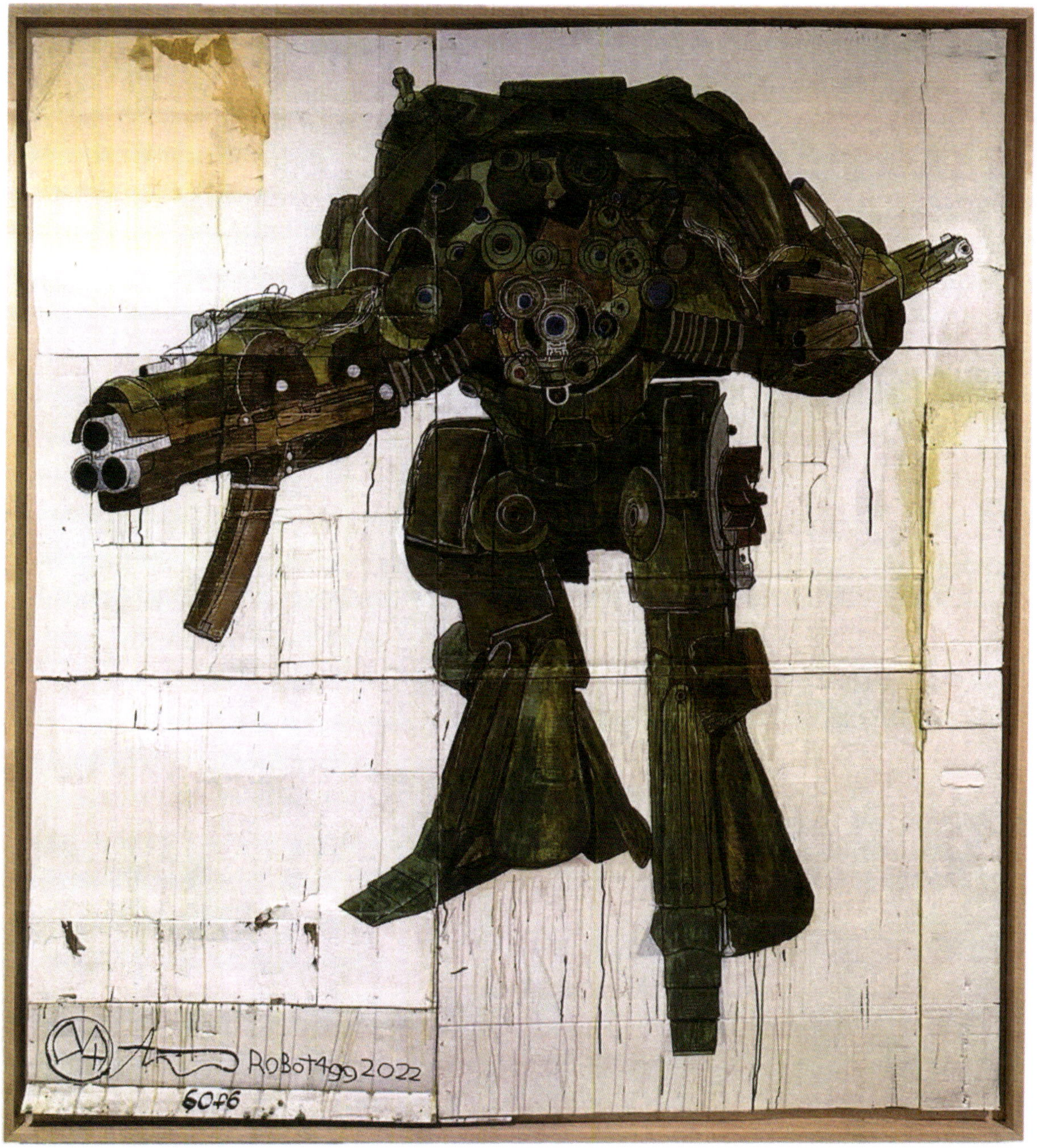

Mr. Martinez's "Robot 499." Alberto Martinez, photograph by Jonathan Goldstein

Julia Morrison, a friend of Mr. Martinez's and a fellow artist, showed him Ms. Sorokin's work, pointing out that, like Mr. Martinez, Ms. Sorokin was a con artist turned artist.

They tried reaching out to her.

"It was impossible to get ahold of her," Mr. Martinez told Insider, speaking of Ms. Sorokin. "So what I did was, I planted some story in Page Six to get her attention."

was a German G3. They were .308 rounds, like *Full Metal Jacket*–a bullet hit the wall, ricocheted, and a fragment went into my leg, right into my thigh, that far from my artery. It fucking hurt like a motherfucker. And I was cursing, 'Puta, Stupido!' I just cursed a stream at him, you don't curse at guys with guns, you know? And back then I weighed 190, I was pretty fit, I dressed in khaki army pants, combat boots, and an oxford shirt tucked in. That was the uniform of Americans down there who had business to do. And I adopted that because no one will stop you if you look like that. People will get out of the way. That's what they look like down there, militarized Mormons. So Gary heard from the neighborhood that something happened at the supermarket."

"Who's Gary?" I asked. "He was a bush pilot I worked with down there in 1986. He rode up on his motorcycle, a really fucked up Harley Davidson (it was a beautiful bike at one point, but he stopped caring about it), and it was belching smoke and he was like 'What the fuck happened?' The soldiers were saying they were going to take me to the hospital. Gary started yelling at them, 'What the fuck are you guys doing, you know who this guy is? You don't want to know who this guy is.' I was like 'what is Gary doing?' Because he's not like that, he's mellow. And he said 'Drive us to the airport.' And they all said no, but Gary picked out the youngest soldier to come with us, and we drove off. And Gary explained to me, 'Those guys were going to take you and fucking shoot you.' We got to the airport, got in the plane, and flew straight to Panama and went right to the US Military hospital in Panama City."

That was an entertaining and very Alfredo-esque story, but I wanted to steer the conversation back to China so I asked about the article that appeared in the *New York Times* in January 2010, in which Alfredo was quoted as calling the Chinese police "idiots."

"So do you think that didn't help our situation over there? Saying in the *Times* that the police were stupid?" This was after an incident around the time of the Olympics, when a maid at the hotel he was staying at called the cops on him. "I was making drawings in my hotel room, it was like Ted Kaczynski goes on vacation. And the cops showed up and said 'standard police check.' I was like, 'nothing is standard about a police check.' I asked them what they wanted, and they wanted to check my room. They looked at my passport and then asked me if I was a terrorist. I said, 'You stupid motherfucker, if I was a terrorist I would have shot you through the door!' I blew up at them. I do have a slight thing towards authority, I hate to admit this, usually I can keep my shit together, but if it goes on too long I get agitated. These guys were plain-clothes cops. They were asking me 'Why do you have all these gun magazines?' I was making gun drawings. So I called Micah (a Finnish filmmaker) and Stacey (Duff, the art critic for *Time Out Beijing*), they were close by and both came at same time. Micah had this gigantic TV camera with a light on it, and the cops were like, who are these people? Stacey started asking them questions in Chinese and they left really quickly. Stacey talked to the manager and he apologized. The presence of the camera saved my ass."

He also had a valid visa at this point. I remembered that in the dead of winter earlier that year Alfredo had gone to Mongolia to renew it. Most people went to Hong Kong or Thailand to do that, Alfredo went to Ulan Bator. "I think I was the first Puerto Rican who'd ever set foot in Mongolia. I should have planted a flag. Everyone was going south, it was a madhouse, and so I did the reverse commute, to Mongolia. No lines at the airport. I was there for two days."

That visa ran out six months later and then there was the *Times* article with Alfredo's less-than complimentary assessment of the police force. "So yeah, I was poking the panda bear with a short stick." For a while we swerved off to discuss just how strange it was to be back in the United States after three years in the Middle Kingdom. "It feels so familiar, but alien. It's weird being able to understand people when you come back. That's one of the great things there in China, not understanding people's conversation. It's like white noise. The culture shock is harder coming back to New York than it is going there. All the stuff that you were used to, you realize how bizarre it is." John Dillinger, Joseph Beuys (a big influence), and Blinky Palermo came up in the conversation, as did Alfredo's adventures during the just-ended Fashion Week. He'd been going to some parties. "I went to a party for new in-house fashion line, Joseph Conteras, I got to the club dressed, you know, not exactly fashion forward, and there were all these fashionistas, it was like *28 Days Later*, they were desperately trying to get in. I went to the pay phone, called the guy inside, and he said to go to the door and ask for Sasha, then say I need to see Tyrone. I asked at the door, did the secret handshake, and we got in. My God, were those girls waiting in line pissed!"

Then a subject was broached that never ceased to figure prominently in our general palavering back in Beijing–women. Specifically the Chinese variety. "It's nice to come here and talk to girls. I became like a hermit over there, which is kind of unhealthy. I was like, why take a shower? There are no girls over there that you can be interested in in that way. That's why guys take showers, to get laid. My whole game is in my language, and that didn't work over there. I realized that having a girlfriend there is like having a pet. Their outfits, the pink, it's like Halloween. I was at this party there and my friend told this girl I have work in MOMA, and they loved that, the branding. The girls were suddenly more interested in me. They were asking me what my Chinese name is, and I would play this joke where I tell them my name is "Shabi" (cow pussy, or just plain stupid) and they would have this horrified look on their faces. They'd call a guy over and he would have to embarrassingly explain, and then burst out laughing. And I realized nobody had ever done a joke like that in China. There's no irony or sarcasm. Have you ever met a sarcastic ant, or bee? It just doesn't exist. I like sarcastic girls. They don't know what the word is. They have to look that up in their little electronic dictionaries."

And then on to another favorite topic, especially if you actually have to experience it, which is that week of totally explosive insanity that is Chinese New Year. "It's like being under shelling in Beirut. People buy fireworks at the corner store that here you would need a professional permit for and a fire marshal. One of the funniest things I saw was one of those Jingbei vans stuffed to the gills with fireworks and the guy smoking in the front seat. I just imagined that if it all lit up and the back doors were open the little JIngbei van would fly down the street like a bottle rocket."

Since Alfredo had gotten back he'd been able to decompress a bit at a friend's parents' house in Pennsylvania, though that proved to be too relaxing. "They're old bohemians. Great old ramshackle house, full of books and paintings. I was relaxing there for a week, making work. I got athlete's foot from Chinese prison and I cured that there, walking around barefoot on the lawn. Near Allentown. But I felt out of place, it was like being in an Abercrombie & Fitch photo shoot, these young, beautiful people and this utopian environment. It's nice but I needed to make money and get back to the city. I needed to get back on the horse."

Related to that was the case of all Alfredo's drawings he'd brought back from China. The only possessions he'd wanted to rescue, they had been brought to the airport by his friend Byron right before his involuntary departure. It's a bit convoluted, but this should get the concept across of how Alfredo lost the majority of the work he'd made in the last year. "I was freaked out because I'd just talked to Homeland Security at the airport. I was nervous, the adrenalin started pumping, and the entire flight back I couldn't sleep, so I was not in my right mind and I was yelling at those guys. But they were cool and I got out after half an hour and I had my drawings. But I had no money. This Dominican livery cab driver gave me a ride to the gallery (The Proposition, which represents Alfredo) but it wasn't open. I gave him my passport and the drawings as collateral since I didn't have any money, and he promised to drop them off at Morris King, the advertising agency. They're nice there; I've known them for a long time. On the way there the driver had thrown out my drawings, though I didn't know that. Why did the guy throw out the drawings? Because he's a stupid Dominican. He thought I was some crazy homeless guy. The guy got paid at Morris King and gave back my

Alfredo Martinez, Artist Who Faked Basquiats and Organized an Anna Delvey Show, Dies at 56

BY ALEX GREENBERGER

August 29, 2023 12:47pm

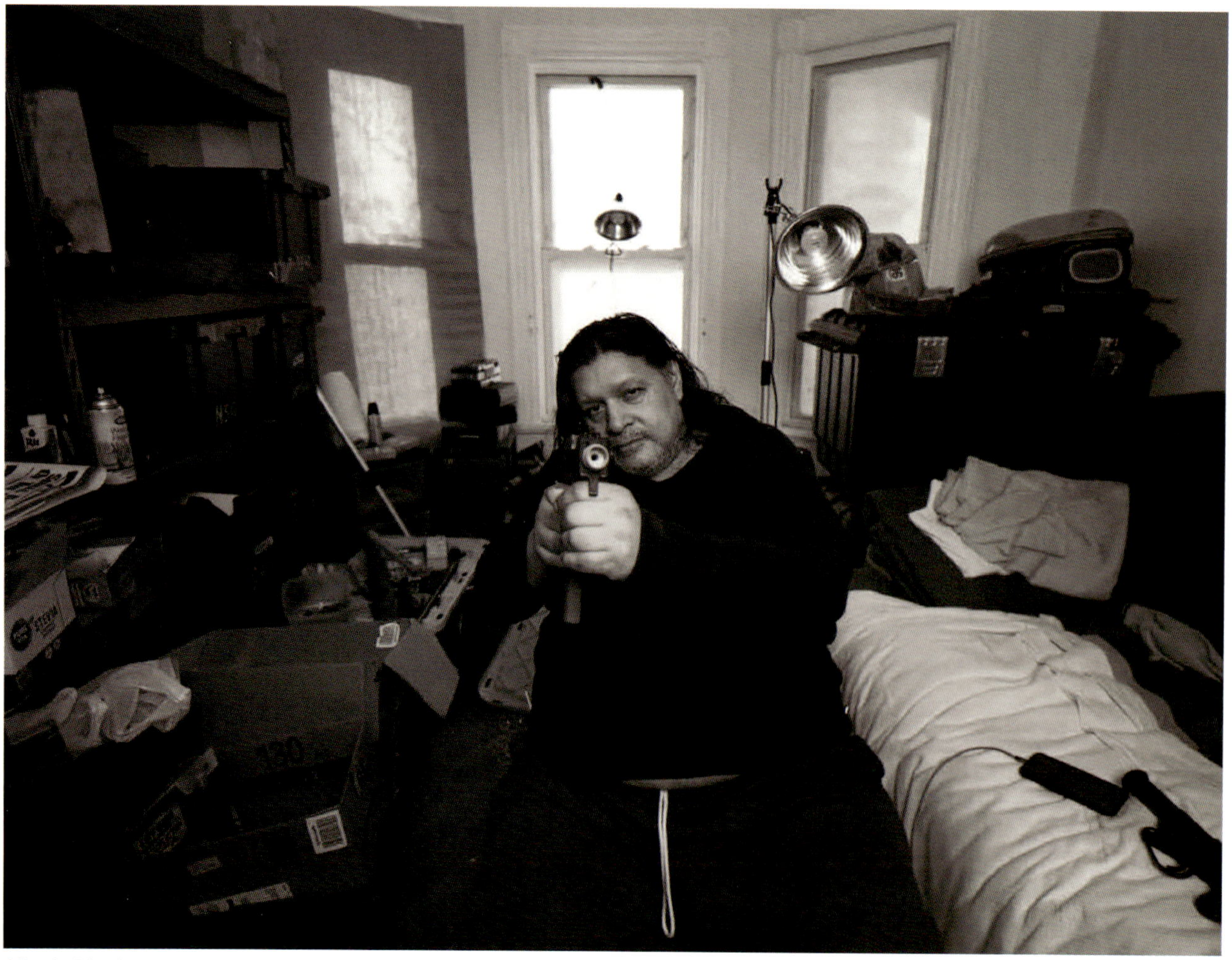

Alfredo Martinez.
PHOTO JOSEPH MILLER

Alfredo Martinez, a New York–based artist who grabbed headlines for faking Basquiat paintings and organizing a show of **Anna Delvey**'s art, died on August 21 at 56, according to various posts on social media, including **one from the actor Adrien Brody**.

Brody called Martinez "an inspiration and a friend who always tried to help me along my path as an artist."

Julia Morrison, a close friend of Martinez who co-organized the Delvey show, confirmed his passing, saying that he had been battling diabetes. She said that Martinez died with multiple film and television projects and a solo exhibition of original works planned, and that a memorial was being organized. His family asked for privacy.

Martinez's larger-than-life persona and art became a source of fascination in New York, where his works about guns found a loyal following. One is currently held by the Museum of Modern Art.

Discussions of his art typically follow mention of his arrest in 2002 by the FBI. Martinez had attempted to sell 17 forged Basquiat paintings that were based on real ones and was given a 27-month prison sentence as a result. Much later on, he claimed that he had forged works by Keith Haring as well.

In 2021, he explained his choice to fake Basquiat's work, saying, "My personal take is perhaps Basquiat was doing a bit of a gag, because his early work was more cartoons, so he wanted to make things for the 'art world,' so his idea was to copy Picasso, who was copying Black art from Africa."

At the time of his arrest, Martinez had already earned a reputation for making art about guns. He had served as a studio assistant to the artist Donald Baechler at one point, and was at the time starting to make a name for himself. Yet he struggled to make a living, at one point even sleeping in a container near the Gowanus Canal, as the critic Anthony Haden-Guest once reported.

While incarcerated, Martinez continued to make art—and even twice went on hunger strikes when guards refused to let him do so, since art was not legally allowed in New York prisons at the time. Using coffee grounds, pen, pencil, and mashed-up pieces of paper, he created images of guns, which were then smuggled out and sold and exhibited by galleries. "His own work was always interesting—it included hand-fabricated guns—but prison has taken it to a new level," Haden-Guest **wrote in *New York Magazine***.

Alfredo Martinez was born April 15, 1967. The *Village Voice* reported that he had labeled his father "a Puerto Rican Archie Bunker" and that his mother was "manic depressive." Martinez had been born in Brooklyn and had run away from his home at age 16.

By the time he was 20, Martinez had begun producing his forgeries. Sensing that they were no longer bankable sometime around 1989, he moved to Brussels and became an arms dealer. Then, when he was 21, he returned to the US and enlisted in the Army, which sent him to Europe. Having flirted with what he called "the loan sharking business" while enlisted, he was returned to the US, where, starting in 1993, he committed to being an artist.

During the ’90s and 2000s, Martinez showed his art around New York and curated gallery exhibitions. He was included in the 1999 P.S.1 Contemporary Art Center exhibition “Generation Z,” which sought to broadly explore the kinds of work emerging artists were making at the end of the millennium. His CV listed appearances in shows at vaunted New York spaces like Exit Art and Pat Hearn Gallery, the latter in an exhibition curated by Diego Cortez and David Greenberg

In 2004, while the dealer James Fuentes mounted a show called “The Unites States of America vs. Alfredo Martinez,” which featured artworks Martinez had smuggled out of prison. The *Village Voice* reported that it had been successful.

Martinez cultivated the mythology that surrounded his celebrity in New York. He claimed to have shot Kenny Schachter, then his dealer, with a blank at the Gramercy Hotel Fair. He spent time in China, and claimed to have met Ai Weiwei there before being imprisoned and secretly tortured after getting in trouble for searching information about guns at an internet cafe. He even ran a shooting gallery in a Tribeca basement with the help of entrepreneur Josh Harris.

In 2022, with the artist Julia Morrison, he organized an exhibition of works credited to Anna Delvey, who had grifted members of the art world and was undergoing a prison sentence for it. “It caught me right in the feels, someone making sarcastic drawings in prison,” he **told *Artnet News***.

Technically, the Delvey works included, featuring vampy versions of herself, were drawn by Martinez, who had essentially willed the show into being by placing an article in the *New York Post* in which he stated that the exhibition should exist. She was not able to produce drawings at such a large scale due to prison restrictions, and so Martinez decided to produce them for her with her permission.

Few other artists represented in the MoMA’s collection can say they have connections to Delvey—or even to have been arrested for faking art. “My career now would be more established if I didn’t waste my time with forgeries,” he told *Cell Vision* in 2021.

ALFREDO LUIS MARTINEZ

Born : 4/15/67, Brooklyn, NY

Education : 11TH grade

Work Experience : 1999 consultant on "Ghost Dog" by Jim Jarmusch

1998-2000 assistant to Rick Washburn, Weapons Specialist

1994-1999 Studio Assistant to Donald Baechler

Solo Exhibitions

2004 Deisel Art Gallery Soho, NYC

2003 THE UNITED STATES -VS- ALFREDO MARTINEZ the Proposition Gallery NYC

1999 WHO DARES WINS Donahue/Sosinski Art 560 Broadway, NYC

Group Exhibitions

2006 GUNS MAI (Museum of Art and Industry of Saint-Etienne), MIAM (International Museum of Modests Arts France

2005 Hello Kitty 30" anniversary Mori Art Center, Tokyo, Japan

A WAR LIKE PEOPLE, curated by Lara Taubman, Shade Projects@ Monorchid Gallery, Phoenix, AZ

2002 Welcome to the Playground of the Fearless, Entropy, Williamsburg, NY

2000 QUIET Broadway, NYC indoor firing range designed by Martinez

I999 Generation Z, P.s 1, 1, Long Island City, NY

Paradise 8, Exit Art, NYC

Surface to Air, 17"'Street Gallery, NYC curated by Chris Kelly

1998 CAMBIO, Sandra Gering Gallery, NYC, curated by Kenny Schachter

Surface to Air I, 17TH Street Gallery, NYC, curated by Chris Kelly

Downtown Arts Festival, NYC, installation

1997 The Experimentors, Lombard Fried Gallery, NYC curated by Kenny Schachter

NY Biennalc,450 Broadway Gallery, NYC

Extremely Refrigerated, Fake Shop NYC curated by Jeff Gompertz Auto Portrait~ Exit Art, NYC

1996 Death of the Death of Painting,480 Broome Street, NYC, curated by Kenny Schachter

1995 Notes on the Way to a Nervous Breakdown. Blackout Books curated by Diane Gibson

Imaginary Beings, Exit Art, NYC

Organic Anxiety, Eighth Floor Gallery, NYC

Freaks, Times Square Gallery,NYC

Doom, installation at Pseudo, NYC

Weapons Show, Exploding Sky, NYC

Way Cool, Exit Art, NYC

intoxication, Max Fish, NYC curated by Carlo McCormick

1994 - 1999 How You Play tbe Oame, Exit Art. NYC

Lei the Artists Live, Exit Art, NYC

Bong Show, Alleged Galle,y, NYC

The Agent Artist, P. S. 1 Long Island City, NY

Skater Angels, Pat Hearn Gallery, NYC, curated by Diego Cortez and David Greenberg

1994 studio assistant to Donald Baechler

SS9We.stZ1!S"t'reetINewYOO.N.Y10011I

I wwwJheproposition.com I 212.24'.2.0035

Dowwntown Arts Festival, NYC, installtion

The Experimentors,Lombard Fried Gallery,NYC curated by Kenny Schachter NY Biennalc,450 BraodwayGallery, NYC

Extn:mely Refridgemtcd,FalceShop, NYC curated by Jeff Gompertz Auto Portrai~ Exit Art, NYC DeathoftheDeathofPaint-ing,480BroomeStreet, NYC,curatedby Kenny Schacht« NotesontheWaytoaNer-vousBreakdown.BlackoutBooks,curated Diane Gibson

Imaginary Beings, Exit Art, NYC

Organic Anxiety, Eighth Floor Gallery, NYC

Freaks,Times Square Gallery,NYC

Doom, installation at Pseudo, NYC

Weapons Show, Exploding Sky, NYC

Way Cool, Ex.itArt, NYC

Intox.ication,Max~Fish, NYC curated by Carlo McCormick

Reviews

2004 Art in America, Sara Valdez

Dazed and Confused, The Art and Artillery of Alfredo Martinez by Dave Calihoun •

New York Magazine, The Hunger Artist by Anthony Haden Guest

Artnet by Walter Robinson

Flavorpill by PaulLaster

Page Six, New York Post, Pen and Clark, john Lehmann

Black Book, The Artist and the Forger by Chris Lee

Artreview, Wannabe Gig Shot is Busted by Anthony Haden-Guest

2000 The New York Times by Roberta Smith, Weekend ''Na'er Do Wells"

1999 Art in America, Import/Export Generation Z: Slacker Than Thou, P.S. 1 by Nancy Princcothal

Zing Magazine, Generation Z

New York Times Magazine, Death of the Death of Painting

The Village Voice, Kim Levin

New York Newsday, Way Cool

New York Daily News, Way Cool

WHO DARES WINS

Installation View

1999

Donahue / Sosinski Gallery

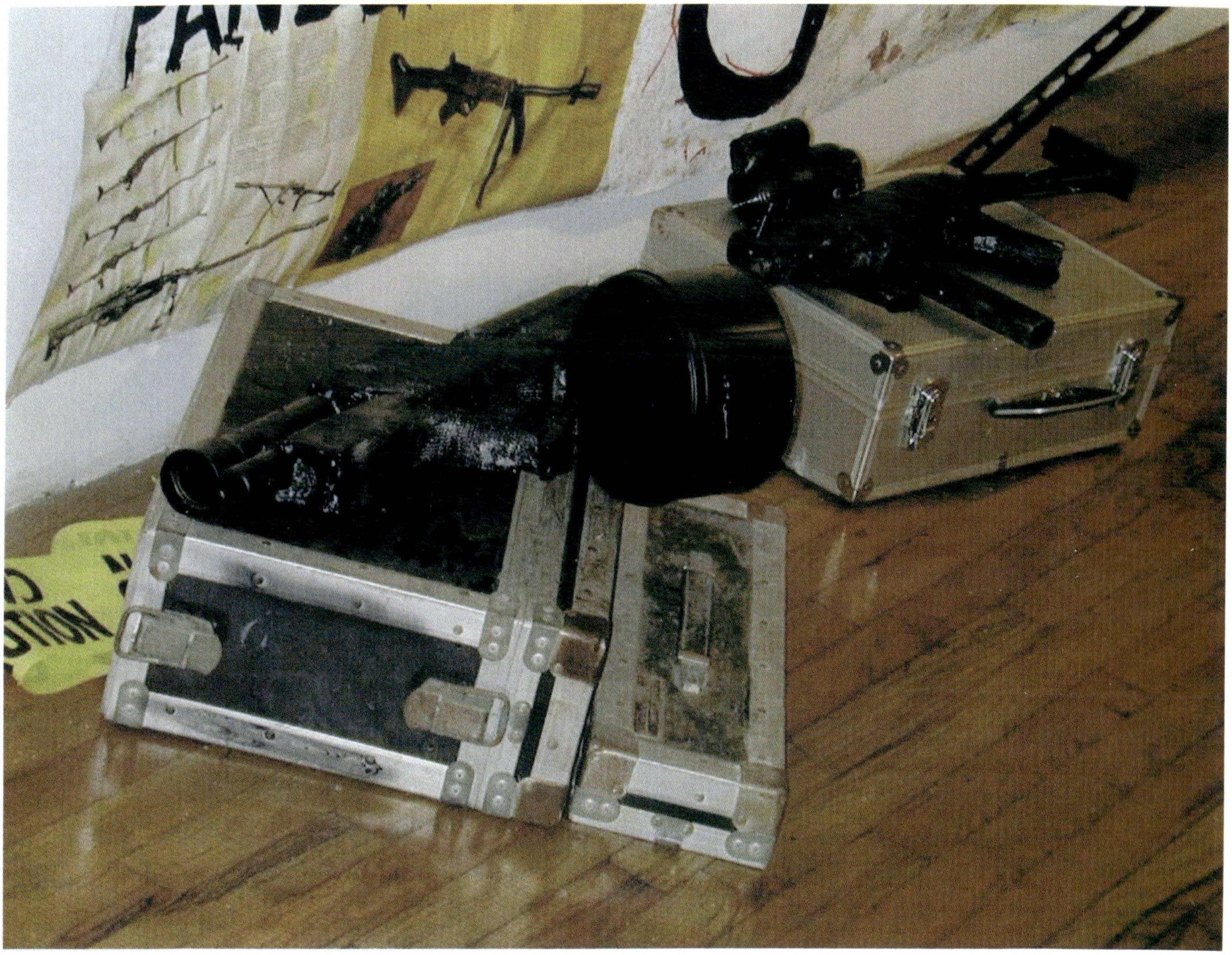

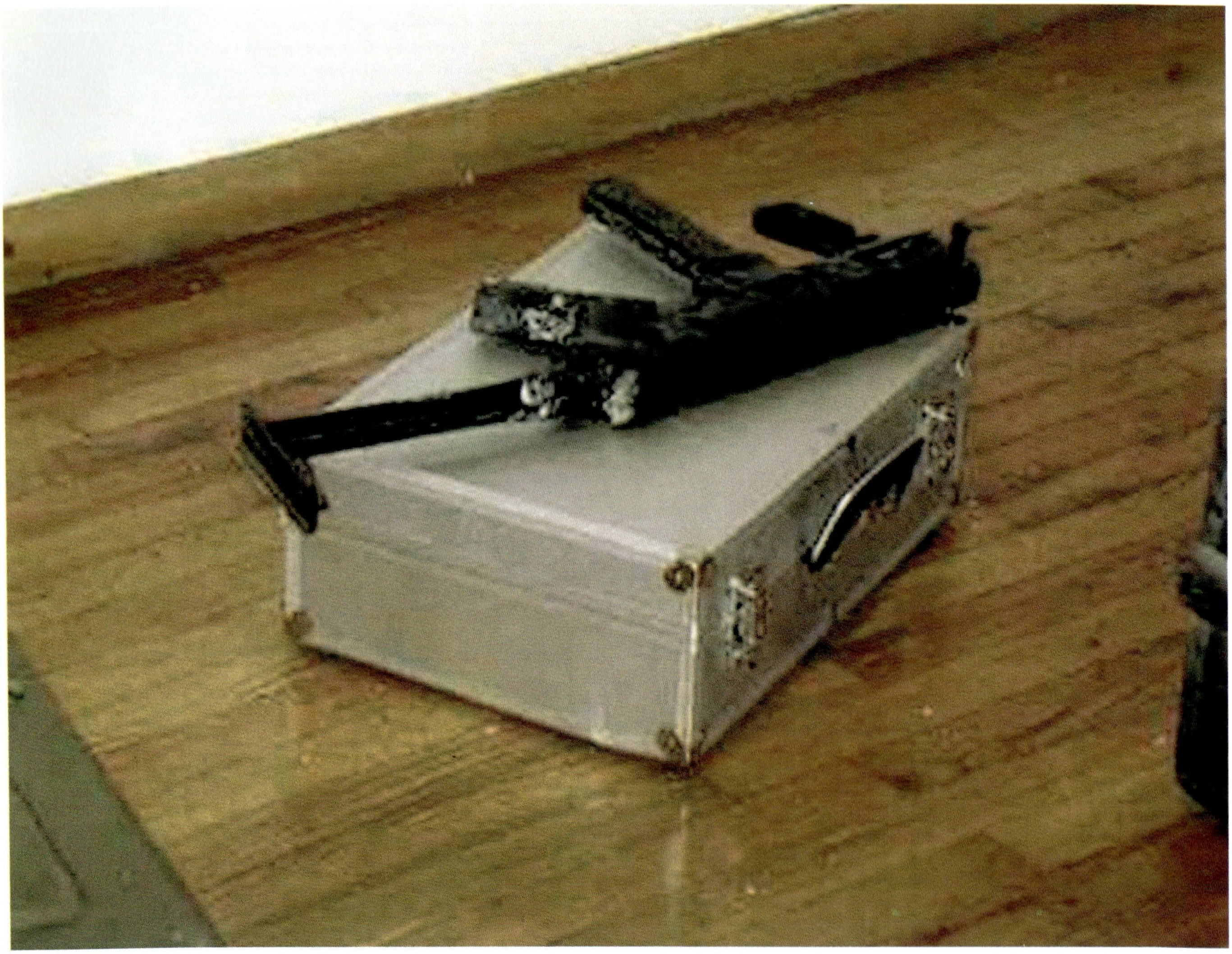

WHO DARES WINS

Installation View

1999

Donahue / Sosinski Gallery